CHURCH CONFLICT

FROM CONTENTION TO COLLABORATION

NORMA COOK EVERIST

Abingdon Press
Nashville

CHURCH CONFLICT: FROM CONTENTION TO COLLABORATION

Copyright © 2004 by Abingdon Press

Library of Congress Cataloging-in-Publication Data

Everist, Norma Cook, 1938-
    Church conflict : from contention to collaboration / Norma Cook Everist.
        p. cm.
    ISBN 0-687-03801-4 (alk. paper)
    1. Church controversies. 2. Conflict management—Religious aspects—Christianity.
I. Title.
    BV652.9.E94 2004
    250—dc22   2004011449

04 05 06 07 08 09 10 11 12 13—10 9 8 7 6 5 4 3 2 1

MANUFACTURED IN THE UNITED STATES OF AMERICA

To all people who address conflict,
not through violence, but through
collaborative means of justice, shared
power, peacemaking, and partnership in
interdependent communities locally and
globally, particularly the United Nations

CONTENTS

INTRODUCTION

Maybe it's the sleepless nights or the knot in the stomach. Congregational leadership used to be so invigorating. But lately—

You love your work. You love the people, most of the time. They respect you, most of the time. You work together with colleagues, staff, and laity, with energy and enthusiasm, most of the time. But then something goes wrong—a word spoken in anger, a misunderstanding, and things turn sour.

Or perhaps the place where you minister is mired in controversy. Habitual conflict has drained the community of strength for, or even interest in, mission. Or perhaps a recent congregational difference of opinion concerning a mission strategy, or biblical interpretation, or your leadership has escalated to the point that people are leaving, or intent on *your* leaving. Whatever the ache or the anguish, each of us at some time, in some way, is called to look seriously, or look again, at the effect conflict has on communities of faith and our role in the midst of it all.

This book is about living together amid conflict. Conflict is part of the human predicament. It is real and seemingly endless. Even the most calm congregation and caring relationship may have conflict brooding just beneath the surface. This book is about *working* together in the midst of conflict. It is possible to move through conflict from contention toward collaboration. Collaboration, as used in this book, is both a strategy to use amid conflict, and an environment that can be established and maintained for long-term life and work together. This book moves beyond living in the midst of conflict; it offers insights and tools to help pastors and professional ministerial and lay leaders discern the nature of conflict and move appropriately beyond contention to collaboration.

When we are in the midst of conflict we are tempted to think it is not *about* us. Surely there are those troubled and troubling people who stir things up. But, of course, we are real, living human beings and our very presence influences the situation. We cannot be merely a neutral force. This book will help each of us discern our own relationship to conflict and the role we can and cannot play in a specific situation. It can be read by oneself, used in a colleague group, in a classroom, or by judicatory leaders helping troubled congregations. The book is written from a Christian perspective and draws on tenets of the faith. It can be used ecumenically as well as within individual congregations. It is intended to provide hope for ways to help create a sustainable ministry that can not only survive but also utilize a variety of strategies to respond to conflict.

Different persons will read this book through different lenses, because of ways they view conflict, because of their personal histories, or because of the nature of the present conflicts they face. This book will help various readers identify their strengths and weaknesses in responding to conflict and will also help them gain the skill to decide which response they should use, depending upon the circumstances. Pastors may read the book for immediate help and personal growth. They also may use it to help a staff, council, or congregation analyze the nature of conflict, look at specific ways to face the conflict together, and gain hope and skill for moving toward a more healthy, collaborative ministry.

Personal Reflection and Collegial Conversation

At the end of each chapter the reader will find a brief section, "Personal Reflection," to help one think about one's own history with conflict and growth in dealing with it. This is followed by another brief section, "Collegial Conversation," which can be used with one's own staff members, or with a group of ministerial leaders from neighboring congregations, or with a church council, or an adult forum, or in a retreat setting.

In addition, there are many questions posed within each chapter. These are not simply rhetorical, but are meant to stimulate reflection or conversation. The inclusion of dialogue by real people is meant to draw forth the individual reader or group's own memories and views on conflict situations.

The participants in dialogue presented in the chapters of this book—now pastors and diaconal and youth ministers—come from many and varied backgrounds, including: volunteer coordinator at a homeless shelter, insurance manager, camp director, volunteer for sexual assault prevention and education programs, outdoor retreat staff director, electrical engineer, oyster farmer, computer sales manager, carpenter, vocational rehabilitation program director, third-grade elementary school teacher, internal revenue service tax accountant, mother, father, medical aide, adult nonreader group organizer, nurse, financial services consultant, nuclear power plant engineer, and theater artist. Readers will find the insights of these people on both conflict and collaboration will stimulate reflection and conversation. Readers are invited also to bring their own rich and varied backgrounds to the chapters of this book.

Content of the Book

Part One: The Nature of Conflict

Chapter 1: Images of Conflict Do we view conflict as a war, a trial, a game or something else? This chapter will provide ways for people to understand what conflict means to them and to others with whom they live and work. People hold many and varied images of conflict. By understanding the reactions of people toward conflict we begin to provide ways to understand one another.

Chapter 2: Types of Conflict One of the most difficult parts of addressing conflict is figuring out what kind it is. Is the conflict over me or inside of me? Is the problem over an issue of church policy or beliefs? Conflict may be intrapersonal or interpersonal. Conflict may revolve around issues, facts, values, goals, or means. There are often many layers to conflict. In a particular conflict we ask, what is going on and why?

Chapter 3: Patterns of Conflict Conflict can be destructive or productive. Escalating conflict may move from disagreement to judgment to a shouting match. Widening conflict may move from a few people to a whole committee to the entire congregation. Conflict may become contagious or even habitual. This book will not attempt to solve all conflict; this chapter offers insight on directions conflict can take.

Chapter 4: Personal History of Conflict How we have handled conflict in the past influences how we are likely to respond today. Early memories of conflict in the family, at school, and at work can guide us in understanding ourselves. What is my history of response? How am I the same? How have I changed? How can memories be healed?

Chapter 5: Roles in Conflict Each situation brings its own complexities and challenges, and its own call for leadership. If a conflict is between me and another person I will not be able to also be mediator. Understanding which role we can play goes a long way in helping us discern the appropriate style for effective ministry.

Part Two: Responses to Conflict

Chapter 6: Avoidance To avoid conflict has sometimes been perceived as being cowardly. But on some occasions avoidance is the appropriate, even the "strong," leadership style. Jesus sometimes refused to engage the crowd: "My time has not yet come." To avoid gives time to gain information, to calm and strengthen the community.

Chapter 7: Confrontation People confront when the stakes are high and when they feel passionately about an issue. Refusing to confront may say that we do not care about the mission or the people. Healthy engagement of differences can strengthen community. But always using confrontation may intimidate and not foster collaboration.

Chapter 8: Competition Those who love to compete are frustrated with those who won't engage. Whereas this approach may work for those for whom conflict is a "game," it is not fun for those who perceive that they will always lose. Our society highly regards competition. What is the place of competition in a community of faith?

Chapter 9: Control Controlling leaders believe they are on top of things, but often conflict moves underground. Responsible leaders need to exercise appropriate authority so that people do not hurt themselves or one another. We should control the environment, not the outcome; maintain a disciplined meeting, but not control people's ideas.

Chapter 10: Accommodation Accommodation involves adjustment of one's own needs and goals; it also involves respect and hospitality to the other. But if only one party always accommodates, collaborative resolution of conflict will not be achieved. At its best, the fruit of reconciliation is mutual accommodation.

Chapter 11: Compromise When a community's only strategy is to compromise, it may never take risks, producing neither clear witness nor fruitful mission. Positively, compromise means living *with* one another in the promises of God. We can learn to listen, to negotiate, and to act, holding one another accountable in mutual promise keeping.

Chapter 12: Collaboration Communities can live and work together in the midst of conflict. When collaboration becomes ongoing, it lessens destructive means of dealing with conflict. Decision making by consensus can serve this goal. Such collaboration means people will be valued, engaged—yes, fatigued—and energized together.

Appreciation

This book has been a collaborative effort. I thank the sixty-two pastors, bishops, diaconal ministers, and laypersons who wrote long and heartfelt responses to inquiry about the need for such a book and the shape it might take. I thank the members of the ninety congregations and their pastors I have visited across this land in the past decade who shared with me their challenges and ever-changing ministries in diverse contexts. I thank participants in my seminary classes, particularly "Community, Conflict, and Collaboration," "The M.A. Colloquium," and "Leaders in Mission" for their engaging conversations about ideas in this book. I give particular thanks to the participants whose dialogue is reflected in the pages of this book (and who chose their own pseudonyms): Liz Albertson, Nicholas D. Cordray, Sarah R. Cordray, Richard Likeness, Kit Obermoller, Connie Baumann Matye, George T. Rahn, Nancy Phoenix Reed, Jim Roth, Thomas W. Smith, Dirk R. Stadtlander, Mackenzie Grondahl, and Kay Wold.

A special thank-you to Richard Likeness, whose partnership in reading and conversing about various drafts of this book was invaluable. I thank Craig Nessan, friend and colleague, with whom I have been privileged to collaborate for ten years, team teaching senior seminarians in "Church and Ministry." I appreciate the faculty and administration of Wartburg Seminary, Dubuque, Iowa, whose work together is truly a collaborative ministry. Special thanks to Jane Sundberg, Mary McDermott, faculty secretary, and to student assistant Daniel Gerrietts for their faithful work.

Finally, ongoing appreciation for my husband of more than forty years, Burton Everist, and for our three sons and their families whose support, particularly in my teaching and writing while living with a chronic illness, continues to be invaluable. Thanksgiving to God for the diverse congregations where I have served as deaconess and pastor, and where I have been a member, for leading God's people in the midst of all kinds of conflict from contention toward collaboration.

PART 1
The Nature of Conflict

CHAPTER ONE

IMAGES OF CONFLICT

Conflict! Is it a mess? An adventure? A maze you cannot find your way through? In the face of conflict do you feel a surge of energy? A knot in the stomach? Exhausted? Each of us has our own image of conflict that can be expressed in a word, a phrase, or shown as an object. Our purpose is to uncover and to explore those unnamed yet very present images so that we can better understand ourselves and our reactions to conflict. In beginning to identify our different images of conflict—perhaps yours is an invigorating sport while mine is a bottomless pit—we can see why we have such different feelings about it and different ways of addressing it. That is at least a beginning of moving from contention toward collaboration.

How did our ideas about conflict come into being? Partly through our own personality; partly through our family of origin, including birth order; and certainly by our experiences with conflict and the roles we play in conflict at various stages of our lives. We will take time to reflect on our own personal experiences with conflict in chapter 4, but it is not too soon to begin to take note of past experiences of conflict as they flash into our minds. The culture and times in which we live also form us and shape our views of conflict. For example, some Asian cultures emphasize addressing one another with respectful formality, even when parties disagree, to help the other "save face," whereas newscasters in the United States seek viewers' attention through a lead sentence such as "They came out swinging," even when a public meeting was calm and respectful.

Our religious beliefs about conflict determine how we approach conflict. Do we believe in evolution of the human species according to the survival of the fittest? If so, the contentiousness of competition is perfectly natural, even necessary, for human survival. Do we believe in a God who punishes people who are not "nice"? If so, we may avoid church conflict. Do we believe in a God who is capricious? If so, we can never know if this God will be angry or merciful. What do we believe about God? How do our beliefs about God shape our approach to conflict and to collaboration? And what do we believe about the church? That it is a place of "nice" people? Then conflict itself might be seen as "unchristian." It is a place of redeemed sinful human beings? Then conflict will be a constant—and God's forgiving grace more constant still.

Conflict: An Image, an Action, a Word

What does conflict mean to you? How does it feel? A group of adults gathered to explore their own understanding of conflict. Listen to the images they shared:

Alan: Conflict to me seems like a cancer. It's not always visible, not always painful in the moment, but it is there systemically, and it can grow.

Bill (holding up a drawing made by a three-year-old child): I see conflict as a mass of emotions, each line being a potential response. I don't know which one to take, where it will lead, or if it can be untangled.

Rose also brought a picture along to the group. Holding up *The Ultimate Kitchen Guide*, she showed a photo of a shiny aluminum pot filled to overflowing with utensils: a spatula, whip, mixer, small bowl, measuring cups, spoons, and a timer. Conflict reminds me of this picture: chaos, a lot of things, but being unable to put them to good use. Craziness!

Ray: I see a dog and a cat fighting. It's hair-raising!

John: For me, conflict has a sharper edge, like a gritty stone in one's shoe.

Marie: My image is similar, like sand caught in your sneaker. Sometimes it's so fine it sticks to you and you can't get rid of it.

Annika: I thought of my congregation just a few days ago. A heated discussion about an issue over which the congregation is deeply divided went on for four and a half hours. My image is of the black hole that our sanctuary became.

Beth: I don't see a black hole at all. I picture a Picasso painting with heads severed from the rest of the body. Or maybe one could see it as Shiva, the Hindu God in whom one sees both destruction and creation. I also think of comic images of Batman's power of encounter with evil: "Wham! Bang!"

The group laughed, pondering the cultural range of those images and then continued.

Francis: I just came from a congregation dealing with conflict through having to answer to authority. Conflict in that situation had more the flavor of a legal battle in a courtroom.

Steve took his turn and stood up, then folded his arms tightly across his chest as if keeping himself in and others out. He just stood there without a word.

Jessie picked up the conversation as Steve sat down: Sometimes it can get pretty rough in a congregation. However, I see conflict in a more neutral light. Conflict is not clearly good or bad. I picture a coin with "avoidance" on one side and "confrontation" on the other. You can flip the coin to either side.

Eileen: I wish I could think of conflict as neutral. I keep feeling afraid. I hear shouting and think about feeling helpless and not being able to think or do anything.

The group sat quietly for a few moments, realizing that for some people, past experience clouds any positive image of conflict. Conflict has been associated with abuse. And then a caring woman picked up the conversation.

Katie empathized with the pain of conflict: I think of a knotted rope, like knots in one's stomach—or like a challenge to untangle.

Darin: Conflict can be very trying. My congregation is in a very unpleasant time. I'm trying to see this time as an opportunity, but it's difficult. I'm trying to connect with other people so I don't feel out there by myself. I see some brightness and some darkness and they seem to be competing forces. There are rays of hope and light. I try to walk in the light.

Hannah added one final image: I picture a group of islands with people on each one. The islands are close enough for bridges to be built between them but they have not been built, so each person is alone and wondering why they are alone.

Living Together with Different Images

Images—some would say metaphors—of conflict provide us with insight about ourselves and one another, how we welcome or avoid conflict, and how each of us engages the conflict process. [1] If we are not aware of our images of conflict, we will not understand how we use it in relationships. Our misunderstandings will multiply. What is conflict for you?

How can we engage in conflict if people don't have the same view? We simply *won't* all have the same view! The goal is not to understand conflict the same way, but to understand just how differently we perceive conflict. Even though some people may resist working on the conflict and the journey ahead may be difficult, exploring the variety of different images with which we work provides a beginning.

Example: A congregation is in the midst of a conflict over retaining personnel. Finances dictate cutbacks. There are personal loyalties, mission goals, and a myriad of other issues involved. People's working definition of conflict shows in the comments about the situation: "This issue is going to consume us" (Alan's view of conflict as a "cancer"). "It's irritating to have to keep going through this" (John and Marie's view of sand or a stone in the shoe). "I hope we can see our way clearly through this" (the image of darkness of Annika and Darin). "I don't want to see anyone hurt" (Eileen's concern that conflict is abusive). "Let's look at the contracts" (Francis seeing conflict in legalities).

Each of these views brings to the table a whole set of assumptions and feelings about the problem and about what this difficulty means to the life of the congregation. If people use these varied images in trying to discuss a conflict, they could create even more misunderstanding or even a stalemate. [2] However, through recognizing and trying to understand one another's perspectives, a group could work creatively on a collaborative approach to their conflict.

Collaboration: An Image, an Action, a Word

In order to move from a contentious toward a collaborative way of dealing with conflict, we need to consider the relationship of collaboration to conflict. Are the two opposites? Do we work through conflict in order to get to collaboration? For our purposes we will use collaboration both as a strategy for resolving conflict and as a sustained environment of working together in a ministerial relationship. In chapter 12, we shall explore collaboration as a response to and a strategy for conflict. Throughout the book we shall discuss collaborative ways of being together as a faith community. In sharing our images of conflict and seeing how these differences can help rather than block a communal approach to a conflicted situation, we have already begun the work of collaboration.[3] People also have varied images of collaboration.

How did the various members of our group view collaboration?

Bill: I see a crew, a team, focused on a common goal. Working together, they can travel through a potentially dangerous situation.

Annika: I picture a team, too, but it's a theater touring team, each adding something of themselves to the common task. Using a theater metaphor, I see a group of people whose work abides in a living script.

Beth: I see people coming together around a table. Collaboration is very difficult. It can be positive, but also very painful.

Rose: I also see people sitting at a table. They are working together on a difficult problem. Maybe they won't come to resolution, but at least there is dialogue.

Hannah had been sitting next to Rose all evening. Now she picked up the picture *The Ultimate Kitchen Guide* that Rose had used to image conflict and said: I had another idea of collaboration in mind, but I can't resist using Rose's picture. I don't see conflict here. I love to cook, so I see all these utensils just waiting to be used together to create a gourmet meal.

Katie: I'm thinking once again of a rope—actually two ropes this time. But they aren't knotted. The two ropes are unlike in thickness and strength, but you can wind the fibers together by wrapping them and thereby increase their strength. That wrapping action is the Spirit.

Eileen: I'm reminded that among your many gifts, you are a weaver, aren't you, Katie?

Ray: My image involves ropes, too. I'm thinking of those who have climbed Mount Everest. We hear of heroic individuals who have reached the peak, but they wouldn't have succeeded even in reaching the first camp without the native Sherpas. And the climbers need to be tied together. And then there's the collaborative wisdom of those who first climbed with those who climb now.

Marie: I, too, thought of mountain climbing. To reach the peak is a huge goal. Some people dropped out along the way, but many of them supported those who did reach the top.

John: That makes me think about space flight competition during the Cold War. Interpersonal conflict is often expressed in similar terms as the "space race": warfare, competition, explosiveness. Tragedies in both countries' space programs led to mutual sharing of research and technology and eventually to building together the space station Alpha.

At that moment *Steve* stood up—as he had done earlier—but this time he reached out his arms and took the hands of those around him. What a strikingly different posture! What a different view of Steve.

Francis spoke up: I picture a group of rabbinical students. They are shouting at one another. You think they are angry, but they are merely expressing themselves. They all know they will have their own space to speak from and they exhibit trust and respect in the heat of passionate discussion.

Darin: I see a highway packed with all kinds of cars. People are traveling to various destinations and being mindful of other people's objectives even if they don't know what they are. We give signals—most of the time—to make sure all are safe.

Jessie: How important it is to bring all our gifts to a collaborative event. When we do, we create a good soil in which we can grow new things.

Alan (who had begun the discussion of conflict with the image of a cancer): I see a healthy body, the healthy Body of Christ with all different organs—members—working together rather than being in dissension.

Eileen: Yes, 1 Corinthians 12 reminds us that with our varied gifts, if one member suffers, all suffer together, and if one is honored, all rejoice.

Does collaboration energize you? Tire you out? Just as we need to be aware of different images of conflict in working together, so too, we need to carefully consider one another's images of collaboration.

The group had already collaborated in building on one another's images during discussion of collaboration. What are the roadblocks to collaboration? Depending upon our image of conflict, we might say, "Things are such a mess around here that we can't clear things up enough to ever get any work done." We might say, or hear someone we care dearly about say, "I feel so hurt, so wounded, that I don't ever want to go to that group again."

Perhaps conflict relates positively to collaboration. We might

> *Images of conflict provide us with insight about ourselves and one another.*

say, "That debate at the meeting last night was so stimulating that I feel ready to move on the ideas and put those ideas into action." Or the entire group might feel, "Honestly confronting the issue seemed to clear the air. It has made room for healing to begin so that this group can once again be healthy."

Beliefs About Ourselves, Culture, and God

What is your belief about God concerning conflict? The gift and goal of life together in the church is working together as the Body of Christ, ministering to a wounded world. We are part of that wounded world; we also inflict many of those wounds. We were created for co-labor and we daily confound that promised reality. As gifts to one another we can be the faith community God has and is calling us to be.

People debate whether culture today is more contentious than in previous generations. We live in a society that has raised argumentation to an art and entertainment form. Seeing people fight sells! Disconnection and alienation, combined with lack of respect and understanding, both contribute to and produce unhealthy conflict.[4] Some people gain from keeping conflicts between people unresolved.

But simply blaming "culture" or "the media" disables us from working to create collaborative communities. Christian beliefs can form a basis for understanding: most Christian church bodies use the Apostles' and Nicene Creeds. Using the three articles of those creeds we can consider the beliefs we confess about God.[5] Each has something to say about the nature of God, our relationship to God and therefore to one another, even—maybe particularly in times of conflict.

The First Article of the Creed

"I believe in God ... creator of heaven and earth." What kind of a God do we have anyway? How were we created to be? If we believe God is a God of chaos, turmoil is the norm. But when we confess that God created a good universe out of chaos, we trust that we were created not to kill one another but for healthy interdependence in the many ways that we are called to live together here on earth. Human beings are created in the image of God, not to imagine themselves to be domineering gods over one another, but to be stewards of the earth and of human community. Living in the image of the God who creates, sustains, protects, and provides, we are created to imagine a richly diverse, just, and collaborative world.

The Second Article of the Creed

"I believe in Jesus Christ . . ." The human predicament is brokenness and alienation from God and from one another. In Christ's death and resurrection we have been freed from bondage for restored relationships. Some people picture atonement only as Jesus' dying to appease the angry Father God. This sole image has been used to justify abusive, violent conflict. The second article focuses first on the birth of Jesus who came to live among human beings in the midst of the most difficult conflict, suffering with us, not to glorify conflict or oppression, but to love and liberate and reconcile.[6] Christ lives to save and to serve, to bind up wounds, and to bring light to our darkness.

The Third Article of the Creed

"I believe in the Holy Spirit . . ." The third article of the Apostles' Creed connects the work of the Spirit with the church, the "communion of saints," "the forgiveness of sins," and "the resurrection of the body." The Spirit gathers forgiven people into communities of faith and connects us as the living Body of Christ for the work of ministry together (co-laboring) in the world. Historically, Christians have at times adopted a "conquest for Christ" approach to mission that glorifies the conflict of war and the resulting subjugation of entire peoples. An alternative image portrays a diverse and reconciled people at the communion table, empowered for a multifaceted mission of sharing God's unconditional love in Jesus Christ.

Even when we share a common faith we can have differing views about the nature of conflict and collaboration.[7] The group continued their conversation.

Jessie said, "I believe human beings are created, 'hardwired' for belonging. We are relational and need regular, intimate, consistent interactions. When we experience such collaborative relationships, we have a deep-seated sense of belonging to one another that can help us deal with the inevitability of conflict. This belonging is not possessive, but rather mutually nurtures, sustains, encourages, and supports us. We need this as much as we need air to breathe."

Steve and Katie shared with each other ideas about the human predicament. Steve said, "Conflict comes from having not only a strongly held personal belief but also an unwillingness to see the situation from the other person's perspective. Conflict happens when people choose to see things only through their set of lenses." Katie added that for her the problem is compounded when the conflict is with someone she cares about. "I am tempted to walk away because I don't even want to hear the scope of our differences."

The myriad of ways we can confound one another in contentious relationships is endless. Moving toward collaboration is never simple. Ray saw collaboration as a gift of the Creator God and the Redeemer, Life-giving God. But Beth said, "I'm still a bit skeptical about seeing collaboration as a warm, fuzzy buzzword that is impossible to enact. Without emotions running high, people zoning out, and the frustrations of conflict there could be no room for collaboration, and more important, for growth."

Bill said, "I see conflict as a birthing room for collaboration. Although we may have the dream of saying, 'Let there be collaboration,' only the God who said, 'Let there be light' can bring forth and sustain collaboration."

Rose drew the conversation to a conclusion: "We were created for communion with God and one another as we celebrate and struggle for unity amid our diversity. Conflict and collaboration are integral components of this celebration and struggle. We rejoice, dance, eat together, question, agree, disagree, challenge, and embrace. We learn. We grow. God is faithful in meeting us during the times of peace and tranquillity and in times of anger, frustration, and disparity. God is faithful in the very messiness of our lives. Even our sin in the midst of conflict cannot separate us from this faithful God."

Personal Reflection

What image do you have of conflict? What image do you have of collaboration? Have they served you well? Are other images emerging? Take some personal time during the week for such reflections. You may want to jot them down or expand your reflections in a journal. Note different kinds of conflict and collaboration around you, in your daily life, and in the news. Note how you react to conflict in your life, in the world, right now.

Collegial Conversation

Talk with someone (in person, by phone or e-mail) with whom you have what you consider to be a good working relationship. How would you together describe it? How did it come to be? In what ways would you say it is collaborative? Does it have its ups and downs? How might you sustain this collaborative relationship?

Notes

1. Joyce L. Hocker and William W. Wilmot, *Interpersonal Conflict*, 6th ed. (Boston: McGraw-Hill, 2001), pp. 16-26.
2. Ibid., pp. 25-33.
3. Images help us picture not only conflict and collaboration, but also ministry. See Donald E. Messer, *Contemporary Images of Christian Ministry* (Nashville: Abingdon Press, 1989). Messer writes that images attempt to blend concepts, mental portraits, and self-understandings. He urges readers to find images that envision and challenge (p. 21). His images of ministry include: "wounded healers in a community of the compassionate," "servant leaders in a servant church," "political mystics in a prophetic community," "enslaved liberators of the rainbow church," "practical theologians in a post-denominational church," and "a public ministry in a global village."
4. Deborah Tannen, *The Argument Culture: Moving from Debate to Dialogue* (New York: Random House, 1998), p. 25.
5. The Apostles' Creed (ecumenical version):
  I believe in God, the Father almighty, creator of heaven and earth.
  I believe in Jesus Christ, God's only Son, our Lord, who was conceived by the Holy Spirit, born of the Virgin Mary, suffered under Pontius Pilate, was crucified, died, and was buried; he descended to the dead. On the third day he rose again; he ascended into heaven, is seated at the right hand of the Father, will come again to judge the living and the dead.
  I believe in the Holy Spirit, the holy catholic church, the communion of saints, the forgiveness of sins, the resurrection of the body, and the life everlasting. Amen.
6. See Mark 10:35-45 and Philippians 2:1-18.
7. Susan M. Lang, *Our Community: Dealing with Conflict in Our Congregation* (Minneapolis: Augsburg Press, 2002). This little book is a workbook for congregations. Although Lang says that one's views of conflict affect how we deal with it, she does not explore various images (p. 27). Her dominant image seems to be "storm" (pp. 67-86).

CHAPTER TWO

TYPES OF CONFLICT

I couldn't sleep last night. I tossed and turned and kept going over the situation."

When conflict won't let go of us, even enough to sleep, we know something is wrong. When we feel the ache of conflict as chronic indigestion, we know it has hold on us. But why can't we sleep? Why the constant stress? We don't want people to have that much hold on our every thought, but they do. We may fear that members of the congregation taking sides will eventually split the church.

The types of conflict are not neatly divided.[1] The situation at church may center around an issue: Should the congregation put on an addition to provide more office space for the staff? However, that *issue* involves *people*. That "staff" includes me, and yes, I take it personally. The planning committee seems bitterly divided about what our mission is. Don't they realize you have to have adequate space for the leaders to work in order to reach out into the community? And if we go ahead with the addition, I know there is going to be division between those who think you shouldn't go into debt no matter what, and others who want to move ahead financing the project over the next ten years. But I don't lie awake thinking about bricks and mortar, or even dollar signs. It's the chair of the finance committee whose face I see. I feel he has a personal grudge against me, as though he is determined to see that I lose. Sometimes he treats me as though I were his child. Actually, he reminds me a bit of my own father, and that troubles me.

Our human nature—avoiding pain, blaming others—often leads a group to conveniently avoid the hard work of dealing with deep issues by assigning the conflict "interpersonal." "It's just a personality conflict." The group can then easily become an audience, even enjoying "seeing *them* fight." Many a leader has been frustrated by being told, "It's just that you two can't get along," rather than the group saying, "We see we have conflict over values here; let's see what we can do about it."

Various types of conflict often are wrapped up in one situation. It would be simplistic to say one needs to figure out the type of conflict before one can do something about it. But uncovering the layers of a difficult situation and distinguishing one type of conflict from another can help us understand our own response as well as open up possibilities for where to go for help, and how we can collaborate on addressing the problem. That may even help us finally get some sleep.

What was a conflict situation in which you felt frustrated? What were the presenting problems? What hunches do you have about other dynamics that may have been present? What things were said that provide clues about misperceptions of the conflict? Helping a group understand the various types of conflict will help them collaborate on addressing it appropriately. Simply knowing the seven types won't settle the conflict over putting an addition on the church building, but it will give the pastor a place to start and perspective for healthy leadership.

Seven Types of Conflict

Conflict can be complex. Even though one cannot easily separate types of conflict, identifying each type can help us understand what is going on. [2]

Intrapersonal Conflict

Conflict goes on inside our own being, particularly over matters of conscience, choice, and well-being. None of us is perfectly healthy, well adjusted, or mature. To put it another way, because of the nature of the human condition—because of sin, rather than fear, love, and trust in God above all things—we hide, or blame in shame and self-doubt. We become anxious.[3] And, we deceive ourselves. Self-deception is a roadblock to dealing with conflict because we cannot see ourselves, others, or God's will clearly. Because we are rarely able to self-diagnose, much less give ourselves good counsel, we need a wise mentor, a spiritual guide, or a counselor. We also need a good friend, but rare is the friend who has the objectivity to help us at a deeper level. A good friend can offer a listening ear, and can be caring and supportive. We need good friends and more. Ministerial leaders do well to find and maintain an ongoing relationship with a guidance counselor, mentor, or with a spiritual guide. A well-trained professional can help us in times of crisis. He or she also will then have a "base line" on which to measure our reaction to new conflict.

No matter what other types of conflict are going on—over issues, between committee members—tending the conflict going on inside ourselves is important, because even though we may not be to blame for the particular conflict, intrapersonal conflict contributes to relational and communal conflict. The turmoil outside contributes to the turmoil inside, and vice versa. We need to be healthy, wise, mature, and spiritually grounded enough to lead in the midst of conflict.

Interpersonal Conflict

Conflict between people is the story of human history! Some congregational conflict is really a personal issue between people, although it may be played out through issues, mission, or ministry. Members, having experienced our care for them, may expect that we will take sides with them against others. Trusting our wisdom, they may depend upon us to fight their battles for them, or "take care" of the opposition so they do not need to. Ministerial leaders often see themselves as pastoral counselors, willing to help people with family or parish conflict; however, we need to beware of being triangulated.[4] We need to resist the temptation to be drawn into the anxiety of the conflict; but we *can* work to set a trustworthy environment for people to deal with their interpersonal conflict, where they feel safe, respected, and heard.

We need to distinguish conflict that is between people other than ourselves and interpersonal conflict in which we are one of the parties. Knowing the difference determines the options of roles we can play. (More on roles in chapter 5.) Leaders have a propensity to assume conflict is between people other than themselves. Usually our personal feelings, identity, or other people's perception of us is involved at least to some extent.

Members of faith communities sometimes expect their leaders to be saints, almost superhuman. And of course we are not. We will have opinions. And we will be tired. When, within the congregation, we are one of the disagreeing parties, the issues are less clear, and clouded by our own feelings. Who can help? Perhaps a wise elder in the congregation. But more likely someone from outside. We may think such interpersonal conflict will just go away. Perhaps—but more likely it won't. It may just become dormant, resurfacing indirectly through another issue, unless it is dealt with for what it is: interpersonal conflict.

Although we have been speaking about individuals, within a faith community one finds similar distinctions between "intra-group conflict," conflicts *within* one group, and "intergroup conflict," *between* and *among* groups. [5]

In discussing the following five types of conflict, in each case we shall use an example about worship and an example about evangelism.

Conflict over Issues: Beliefs

A congregation may face the controversial issue of what kind of music is acceptable to use in worship. Their *beliefs* shape the issue: What is worship? What is the nature of the church? What do they believe about God? A congregation may face conflict over the issue of evangelical outreach: What do their beliefs say about sharing the faith? And with whom? Do they believe outreach includes working toward social justice as well as preaching the Word of God?

Our calling as leaders of faith communities includes creating and maintaining a place where people holding a range of beliefs on issues can work together in the midst of those differences. This may be a challenge because people of faith hold beliefs about worship and evangelism strongly. How can we be expected to create space for those whose beliefs differ from our own? Do we ever state our own? Are some issues not up for vote?

Within churches there are widely differing views on the role of governments and national policies, economics, race, and more. These may not be played out as much in the theoretical as in the specific. For example, the issue of "Should the United States flag be in the sanctuary?" may appear on a council agenda only after one group bought and placed a flag by the altar and another group removed it. Whether people simply say strong words to one another or act on them, the conflict can be very real.

How conflict over issues is resolved depends upon the church; how conflict over issues is resolved helps shape that church for years to come. In some churches theological issues might become church dividing. What about issues where differences cannot be tolerated? A church does have boundaries to their beliefs. If some people debate the physical resurrection of Christ, or the inclusion of people of all races in the church, won't that place them outside the parameters of the faith? (Note that even "obviously clear" issues may not have been so clear just a generation ago.)

Conflict over Facts: Truth

With the issue of worship, a congregation may have a conflict over facts. In the matter of church music, for example, the music director begins using praise choruses. Some members say to the pastor, "That music is turning everybody away." Just how many members really *are* staying away because of the different type of music? And is the number of new members attracted, as reported by the music director, exaggerated? In the matter of evangelical outreach, a congregation may disagree on their definition ("truth") of the term *evangelism*. Is it calling people to a "decision" for Christ? Is it invitation to church? Is it outreach through social mininstry?

In the heat of a battle, people may say things they don't mean, or that they will later regret. But, perhaps they *do* mean them (even if they later regret the tone of voice they used). When John accuses Jason of lying, he may very well believe Jason *did* lie. John's version of truth and Jason's differ.

Isn't truth, truth? Not necessarily. The two men may have witnessed the same incident, or been at the same task-force meeting, but seen things through different eyes. The way we see is conditioned literally by our *point of view,* where we are standing. How do we help people identify their point of view? We can set trustworthy places in which people tell their histories, explain their frame of reference. We can practice listening skills. We can simply learn to say, "I don't think I understand your perspective. Where are you coming from?" We also differ on interpretation of the facts. Our different view of interpretation of scripture may depend upon our belief about biblical authority.[6]

How, then, can we ever determine what is truth? By acknowledging that we never have "just the facts." God is truth and acts truthfully with us. We can pray for careful discernment, and we can be willing to seek out various "truths" from various sides of an issue. It will mean taking time to search out information and delaying decisions until that is done. Such a procedure is not *avoiding* conflict, but collaborating on finding enough "truth" to resolve the issue. Careful dialogue includes not just saying what each of us believes is true, but in joining our perspectives into a more holistic picture so that together we can move forward with greater communal understanding.

Conflict over Values: Worth

In the matter of worship music, conflict arises over the way people *value* different kinds of music. In regard to evangelical outreach, people *value* differently the worth of certain projects—or people.

As Christians live out their faith in daily life, they make many decisions. Those decisions are based on values. Values permeate the ways we interpret life and relate with one another. We might assume that all members of a faith community who believe in the same God and confess the same creeds hold the same values. But that is not necessarily so. People hold differing values in regard to money, parenting, time, and so much more. How does conflict arise over values? Although church council members all agree that God needs to be central in their lives, they may differ on the decisions they make concerning the use of God's gifts of time and possessions. Kevin negatively judges Brian spending so much time on the golf course, particularly since Brian spoke against supporting the youth group in their two-week trip to a national gathering. Ruth wonders why Tiffany dresses the way she does at worship, and Tiffany can't understand why Ruth became so upset when her quilters group was told they could not leave their supplies out in the fellowship hall.

Our values are based on our sense of worth: worth of time, property, money, people, or ourselves. "What is it all worth?" "Is my effort worth it?" "Am I, or my opinions, of any worth?" Congregations face conflict in regard to race, ethnicity, and gender. People's values may differ according to generation, economics, class, and education. Even though "class" or "values" may never be mentioned, a conflict plays out accordingly. How can we work together when we differ so greatly in regard to values? Do we need to hold the same values if we are to engage in a common mission? [7]

Conflict over Goals: Mission

In the matter of worship music, the congregation may have a conflict over the *goal* of worship: the praise of God, filling the pews, or being "inspired." (Those goals do not exhaust the list nor need they be mutually exclusive.) In regard to evangelical outreach, parishioners may disagree on how many people they want to reach or whether the goal of a project is to gain new members or in general to be of service in the community.

Surely we all are committed to the mission of Jesus Christ. But what is that mission? To win souls for heaven? To work for a just society here on earth? And where is that mission to be? Within the church community? In the parish neighborhood? Around the globe? Our conflict over mission shows up through budgets and buildings projects, time commitments and staffing decisions. When dollars are scarce, congregations often turn inward, cutting out line items for global or regional mission. Mission shrinks. When a faith community is struggling with conflict within, they may focus on a far distant mission as a way of avoidance. Mission becomes a diversion. When people lack ability or will to work through a doctrinal or ethical issue, some people may signal their disagreement by withholding funds for certain projects. Mission becomes the scapegoat.

We may not agree on the form or even the direction of mission. We can, however, trust that we are called to Christ's mission. In carrying out that mission, or, as is often the case, many *diverse* missions of a faith community, Christ builds the church, conflict and all.

Conflict over Means: Ministry

In regard to worship music, a congregational conflict might arise over whether to serve the community by employing only excellence (even if that means accepting only those people who pass a musical audition), or to minister by using the gifts of all, whatever they may be. In pursuing evangelical outreach, a congregation may agree about the mission goal, but fight bitterly about what resources of people and money to use.

Ministry is not merely a means to a goal. Ministry is a gift of God, a way of living and serving in relation to the neighbor. The Body of Christ is made up of many differently abled people. With differing gifts we are called into a variety of ministries within the faith community and in our daily lives in the world. Why do we become conflicted over such diversity rather than welcome it as co-laboring in Christ?

Conflict makes us territorial: "I know 'your ministry' with the food pantry is important, but it's just that I care so much about the young people that it's difficult to understand why the youth room is stored with food, leaving no room for 'my ministry.' " When we consider that all of our ministries are centered in Jesus Christ we may be able to celebrate one another's ministries even if we are not directly involved with them.

In daily life, our ministries may take us in very different, even opposing, directions. Two church members care about peace in the world, but Rachel believes that goal will be reached by forming a peace coalition to challenge governmental systems whereas José wants to work within the system by writing letters. Can Rachel and José be in the same congregation? Will one need to leave to find a more "conservative" or more "liberal" church? Refusing or neglecting to learn about one another's ministries in daily life does not solve the problem. When we dare to explore the differences, we may find that even though Jason is in marketing and Russ is a consumer advocate they share core biblical beliefs.

Helping a group understand the various types of conflict will help them collaborate on addressing it appropriately.

Since each faith community faces conflict, we might as well differ over things that really matter in the world such as public policy on gun control, education, or the environment, and see how our faith translates to ministry in daily life, instead of just arguing over what color to paint the church basement. There is room within the Body of Christ for many ministries.

Conversation on Understanding Types of Conflict

Jessie: I recently spent time in a two-point parish in western Kansas. For many years this small parish could sustain itself, but not now. Two years ago some members had pushed hard for closing this church and merging with another. It was a bitter fight and the merger was defeated by seven votes. Some forty-five people (more than one third of the congregation) left. This conflict caused friction not only between the two congregations, but also within extended families. The conflict involved a difference in values, a difference in beliefs, and a difference in means. It involved intrapersonal and interpersonal relationships. Ranchers are feisty, can-do people who get their pride up whenever anyone tries to tell them they can't do something. Yet privately, several remaining members admitted their church was dying. To admit that meant they had to admit their mortality, too. So no one ever talked about it in a group. It was very sad.

Alan: When I reflect upon cases of interpersonal conflict— conflict over values, beliefs, goals, and means—I realize that these are often accompanied by feelings of uneasiness, confusion, and anxiety inside my own self. Intrapersonal conflict is common as I discern sources of conflict.

Rose: I've experienced intrapersonal conflict being projected into interpersonal conflicts.

Steve: I recall a conflict with a dear friend over homosexuality. Not only did we disagree on the subject, but also I think we differed on what type of conflict it was. I believe my friend would call it a conflict over facts or "truth." I would classify my stance on homosexuality as a matter of belief.

Hannah: I've been trying to think of a situation when the conflict itself is positive. I am a member of an adult Bible study that over two years has developed a cohesive, trusting environment. Do we all agree? Rarely! However, our conflict regarding "truths" from scripture contributes to much growth and learning.

Beth: Learning to name the type of conflict is essential in finding the root of conflict; then the true work of reconciliation and collaboration can begin. One of the most frustrating places of conflict I have experienced involved the goals and mission of a particular agency. As part of my position I was to articulate the mission to others. But the programs I was developing did not match the vision of the management. The work put in was futile, because I came to see the goals and mission of the volunteer programs were not congruent with the overall mission of the agency.

The group went on, each sharing his or her own experiences of conflict. Understanding the different types of conflict can help a faith community move from confusing contention toward clarity and collaboration.

Finally *Bill* said: This makes me think of Moses and Jethro, his father-in-law (Exodus 18:13-27). I have often heard this text used to describe the need to delegate authority and build teams within a ministry setting. Yet as I reflect on types of conflict, I think of Jethro's advice from a new perspective relative to interpersonal and intrapersonal conflict. Jethro confronted Moses: "What is this that you are doing for people?" reminding Moses that his call was to represent the people before God instead of sitting as judge, settling disputes among the people "from morning until evening."

Even though it would be inappropriate to lay contemporary research on "types of conflict" as a grid over biblical texts written thousands of years ago, the story of God and God's people in scripture is full of intriguing complexity for us to ponder.

Reflecting on the types of conflict, what new insights do you see in:

- 2 Samuel 12:1-15
- Mark 7:24-30
- Mark 8:31-33
- Mark 10:17-22
- 1 Corinthians 11:17-34

What other biblical texts come to mind?

Personal Reflection

Prayerfully consider some of your own intrapersonal conflict, particularly during times of stress. Are you more likely to become anxious when conflict is over beliefs, truth, worth, mission, or ministry? Consider keeping a journal noting which types of conflict reoccur frequently and how you feel about them. Use the time and resource to select and regularly spend time with a trusted mentor or counselor. Make a habit of dealing with intrapersonal conflict as it comes along, rather than only in times of crisis.

Collegial Conversation

Take one conflicted situation in your context. It will no doubt be full of complexity. Analyze it from the perspective of the seven types of conflict. How do your perceptions of the conflict differ? Talk further. As you clarify the different types of conflict present, sort out ways to begin to deal with the situation. Dealing with conflict will never be easy, but continue to talk and share perspectives as you work this time, noting ways you can gain insight and skill for the conflicts that inevitably will come again.

Notes

1. Joyce L. Hocker and William W. Wilmot, *Interpersonal Conflict*, 3rd ed. (Dubuque, Iowa: William C. Brown, 1991), pp. 11-12. Hocker and Wilmot describe conflict from a communication perspective as "an expressed struggle between at least two interdependent parties who perceive incompatible goals, scarce resources, and interference from the other party in achieving their goals" (p. 12). Intrapersonal issues are at play in the nature of interdependence.

2. Various authors name and rank types differently. For example, see Marlin E. Thomas, ed., *Transforming Conflict in Your Church: A Practical Guide* (Scottdale, Pa.: Herald Press, 2002), pp. 24-26. This guide presents a pyramid, from the bottom to top: facts, methods, goals, and values. Keith Huttenlocker, *Conflict and Caring: Preventing, Managing and Resolving Conflict in the Church* (Newburgh, Ind.: Trinity Press, 1988), refers to "personality-centered conflict" and "principle-centered conflict" (pp. 83-92).

3. Arthur Paul Boers, *Never Call Them Jerks: Healthy Responses to Difficult Behavior* (Bethesda, Md.: Alban, 1999), p. 51. Boers explores both acute and chronic anxiety.

4. Ibid., pp. 29-56. Triangulation occurs when two people become anxious and in an attempt to deal with their conflict and triangulate a third party. Pastors are particularly prone to triangulation because of their close, often care-giving relationship to families. Transference, countertransference, and projection also play roles in interpersonal conflict.

5. Thomas, *Transforming Conflict in Your Church*, p. 24.

6. See David J. Lull, "Living Together Faithfully with Our Different Readings of the Bible" in Norma Cook Everist, ed., *The Difficult But Indispensable Church* (Minneapolis: Fortress Press, 2002), pp. 93-104.

7. See Penny Edgell Becker, *Congregations in Conflict: Cultural Models of Local Religious Life* (Cambridge: Cambridge University Press, 1999). Becker's very helpful book provides case studies of various types of congregations. Differences among people over local values means they engage in conflict differently.

CHAPTER THREE

Patterns of Conflict

H old on there, I think this debate is getting out of hand."
   "I came here to deal directly with you on this issue, but
   now you're making accusations about my character."
Who has not had this experience of a conflict becoming ugly?
However, sometimes we may hear said—or hear ourselves saying—
"Now I think we're getting somewhere. I'm certainly glad we were
able to talk about this" or "What seemed like a big issue between us
now seems small; our differences seem manageable."
   Conflict may be tolerable, even a welcome energizing event,
but what if it continues to grow out of control? This may be the
most frustrating and frightening part of conflict. Just as a small
fire may give warmth or cook food, what happens when the
entire room, or building, or neighborhood catches fire? What if
one can no longer contain the fire—or the conflict?
   This assumes, however, that the image we have of conflict
likens it to a fire.

The Movement of Conflict

   Conflict is not static. One can discern patterns in people's conflict.
Conflict moves in various directions. *Destructive* conflict spirals
downward. *Productive* conflict moves from contention toward collaboration. Conflict spreads in a variety of ways. *Escalating* conflict
moves from disagreement to judgment. *Widening* conflict moves from
a few people, to a whole committee, and finally to the entire congre-

gation. Conflict may become *contagious*, infecting an ever greater

> *Conflict is not static. It increases, diminishes, and changes.*

number of people, or making some people feel worse just when some finally feel better. Some congregations have a history of *habitual* conflict. No matter how bad things have become, empowered by a faithful God who has taken the ultimate conflict to the cross, we can participate in transformative and even creative conflict.

Destructive and Productive Conflict

Although productive and destructive conflict cannot be totally separated, looking at the characteristics of each can be helpful.[1] What may seem productive to one person may feel destructive to another. What may seem destructive for a while, in the end may actually be productive. Likewise, as a conflict drags on, draining the group's energies, what might have been productive at first ends up destroying the group's passion for mission. Leaders play a significant role in helping direct conflict from contention toward collaboration. Here are some characteristics of destructive conflict and productive conflict.

Characteristics of Destructive Conflict
- Voices are silenced and people avoid one another regularly.
- The atmosphere is one of sadness, apathy, or merely strained civility.
- People gather in clusters to discuss issues outside regularly scheduled meetings.
- People harbor resentments, remembering when they were slighted.
- Creative energy has been replaced by acrimonious rancor.
- Rumors lead to suspicion and shunning.
- Members are dissatisfied with outcomes, feeling only that they have lost.

- Faith is quashed and people leave not only the congregation, but never return to any church.

Characteristics of Productive Conflict
- People feel their voices, although diverse, are being heard.
- People's fears are being addressed and beginning to be allayed.
- People are growing in courage, confidence, and a positive sense of self.
- People are seeking to become more informed about various options and understand one another better.
- People are willing to share power.
- The atmosphere is stimulating and people begin to care more about issues and people.
- People are feeling energized by the encounter and want to continue working on the issues.
- People are demonstrating faith in a God active in human encounter.

Connecting Images and Direction

We began this chapter on the directions conflict can take with the image of *fire*. How congregation members view the direction conflict is taking, and whether or not it is productive conflict, is related to the various images people hold concerning the conflict (as well as to the type of conflict as discussed in chapter 2).

If conflict is a game, increased engagement may produce more excitement. As anyone who has been involved in sports knows, as the game goes on, competition increases. Even those who may have been playing merely for fun discover that as they play the game the game begins to play them. They not only try harder, but they try harder to win. The folk across the net (across the room) can become not simply "playmates" but "opponents" and even bitter rivals.

Another phenomenon needs to be noted: the audience factor. When conflict is viewed as a game, people may become engrossed in watching people compete. They become spectators; increased combat contributes to the "entertainment" value. Cheerleaders chant slogans (the "Budget Breakers" versus the "Old Fogies"). When the game is over, loyalties remain (e.g., to various congregational staff members) and the audience may find themselves waiting for the next match.

If, however, in a congregation the conflict is expanded in a way that many people become capable players, each person's gifts are needed, not to fight one another to win, but to exercise muscles and grow in skills of collaboration. This experience can be energizing, even enjoyable.

Leadership—good "coaching"—is essential. The leader will help the group discern the type of conflict. Are people dealing with values, goals, or interpersonal matters? In order for conflict actually to be enjoyable, there needs to be agreement on what the "match" is about. The leader will need to help the group carefully set time and place boundaries and agree upon "rules." To carry the metaphor further, if the pastor is viewed as "coach" of only one "team," another wise person will need to serve as "referee." [2]

If conflict is a mess, people no longer enjoy being at church or with one another. The conflict may have begun in just a section of the congregation. But the little mess has spread and no one has the energy to clean it up. Sometimes people have lived so long in the "mess" of conflict that they can no longer remember when it was otherwise. But newcomers to the congregation do notice, and rarely want to come very far in the door.

However, when the "stuff" of church conflict is in full sight where it can be no longer hidden, one might as well get everything out in the open so that things can be sorted out. Such a project is not fun to do all by oneself. One can become resentful if one always has to clean up the mess that other people make. Pastors and lay leadership can become very fatigued when they are left to pick up the pieces after a congregational conflict. But if such conflict can become a collaborative project, then collectively people can get things out on the table, decide what needs to be discarded, and what, once sorted out, can be kept, even treasured.

There still will be disagreements over values of what is important to get rid of and what is not, but if the group sees the task through to completion, the new fresh environment will be a place where all can work together. Getting a bit dirty and perspiring is worth it when one sees the results. The group may develop some new disciplines of "sorting things out" on a regular basis by asking, "How are things going?" "Are there some issues we need to tend before we go any further?" The goal is to set and maintain an environment where it is healthy to live together.

Use your images of conflict and expand the metaphor: What happens destructively if conflict grows? What could happen productively using this image?

- If conflict is a weed . . .
- If conflict is a thunderstorm . . .
- If conflict is a trial . . .
- If conflict is . . .

Spreading Conflict

Whether one's image of conflict is a mess, a trial, a weed, or something else, we know that when conflict spreads, we become anxious and confused.[3] We may even panic and look for a way out of our leadership role. Fight or flight, adversarial or appeasing responses are insufficient.[4] We shall examine more thoroughly responses to spreading conflict later; at this point it is helpful simply to understand just which way things are going.

Escalating Conflict

It all started out over whether the committee should buy a new computer for the church office, but then things got out of hand. Soon Sam and Kurt were not only disagreeing about information regarding computers, but competing about where to make the purchase. Then Sam said Kurt "didn't know what he was talking about." Kurt retorted, "You always think you're an expert on everything. That's why I don't like working with you." To which Sam, storming out, said, "Then just forget it. I resign from this committee."

There are many reasons for conflict to escalate. Perhaps Kurt didn't really want to work with Sam on the task of purchasing a computer. Perhaps Sam wanted off the committee anyway. Perhaps Sam and Kurt have some history of conflict between them and so any decision they have to make together escalates beyond what they intend. Perhaps—

Conflicts in a relationship escalate when parties are unable or unwilling to deal with differences as they arise.[5] Sam and Kurt were not able to deal with the computer issue. Their conflict escalated to the point of saying things they may later wish they had not said. Committees that are comprised of people with a healthy range of opinions can get into a fight about values and then about ministry and finally about their common mission together. Time apart can allow things to simmer down (if conflict is imaged as a pot boiling over). We need to be willing and able to recognize when conflict is escalating dangerously, and this may not be easy, except in retrospect. By maintaining a nonanxious presence and perspective ourselves, we may be able to help a group keep things in perspective. Through prayer, which keeps us centered, and by seeking wise counsel, we may learn when to bring conflict back to proportion, as well as when to allow some escalation, in terms of deepening it, in order to address real issues.

Widening Conflict

The scope of conflict can broaden to other issues, other people, and even other churches. Sometimes such widening is unavoidable. It may even be helpful. A conflict can be dealt with in too narrow a fashion, which may exclude others whom the issue affects. However, it can also be widened needlessly, taking the time of those who have no responsibility in the issue. For example, a conflict over the appropriate training of acolytes arises in the altar guild, but the pastor realizes it should really involve the broader worship committee. By the same token, a disagreement about who changes the altar linens need not involve the entire worship committee. Likewise, a conflict over change in the time of Sunday morning worship should not stop at the altar guild or worship committee but be brought before the entire congregation. A farsighted pastor can help broaden or narrow the conflict up front rather than waiting for it simply to spread on its own.

How and when should leaders purposely widen the parameters of the conflict? When the issue of how to spend memorial money that Mr. Garcia had willed to the congregation seeped out in all directions, even a local merchant stopped the pastor on the street and asked what the congregation was going to do with the windfall. (Even rumors about the *size* of the memorial had grown with the widening conflict.) The president of the administrative board considered carefully how to expand the issue to the whole congregation. The meeting he called was short and mainly for the purpose of setting the rumors straight. The benevolence committee shared an appropriate amount of information. (For members unable to attend, and for the record, the information also was put in the form of a letter.) The congregation welcomed opportunity to talk and collaborated on how to prevent further communication glitches. If the growing conflict had been widened only impersonally, people in the wider circle would not have had the opportunity to raise questions together.

Interpersonal conflict between church staff or committee members should not be allowed to widen to the entire congregation. What starts off as a conflict between Ben and April could quickly spread with clusters of people taking sides. A pastor or council president could serve as a calm presence offering counsel to help the parties deal with the issues so as to retain their respect and dignity while they gain perspective on improved ways of relating.

What is the conflict about and where should a group go with it? How does one know if an argument about a tuna sandwich is really about something much deeper? People may be talking at one level when the conflict has already widened. Wise leaders will offer care to troubled and troubling individuals and discern the need for taking the matter further. Sometimes, however, conflicts can grow when they really were about only a tuna sandwich!

Contagious Conflict

Can one catch a conflict as one catches a cold? Can one become immune to conflict? Colds and flu are so common that rare is the person who doesn't fall sick one or more times a year. Simply put, conflict can be contagious and no one is immune.

> *Can one catch conflict as one catches a cold?*

So how is conflict contagious? And should we simply stay away from "sick" people? Realizing the human condition, and that, as the old hymn goes, we all have "sin-sick souls," believing that we are immune will lead only to self-deception. Each of us can be a carrier of conflict, through gossip, triangulation (an attempt by one of two parties to draw in a third to take his or her side or handle the conflict for him or her), or any number of maneuvers.

We can become somewhat immune to the disabling *effects* of conflict by trying to avoid contact when we realize we are not in a healthy state ourselves. We may need a respite in order to get well enough to go out into the community without infecting more people. One can isolate the infected in some regards. The entire community needs to work on building up resistance to deadly infection. The community also can learn to care for one another on the road to recovery.

Conflict can spread through a congregation slowly or like lightning. David is hurt by Melissa's remarks and shares his pain the next time his small group meets. Although the group has guidelines on confidentiality, this situation seems different, beyond the bounds of such guidelines, and so the members, hurting for David, share that pain with others. Soon Melissa and David's difficulties have become an issue for Sue and Rachel and John and Jacob and Jerry. Then, Jacob and Jerry get into a fight of their own about how to help Melissa and David. This story took only days to spread; however, the process can often take months—with the story changing with each retelling. The contagious effect can begin with one small incident but eventually make an entire community ill.

People with the initial complaint may receive the attention and care of the community. Those few may soon feel better, because tending those with insistent complaints can take enormous amounts of energy and time. The "strong" ones are left exhausted and now suffer themselves. [6] Changing plans to tend complaints may be well worth the group's time, unless the pattern repeats itself time and time again, in which case conflict becomes habitual.

Habitual Conflict

We learn from our actions, and actions shape how and what we learn. When a couple, whether in marriage or in a team at work, find themselves fighting regularly over a variety of issues, but using the same pattern, they have developed a habit of conflict. When a community over the years finds itself in a stalemate in decision making, their habitual conflict impedes mission. In such a community the players in the game may change, but the game goes on. Different people come to the bargaining table but very little ever moves off the table. The group seems more content to just sit at that table, arguing rather than feasting. And they are stuck in their seats, petrified or too angry to move out toward other serving tables in ministry in the world beyond. It is safer and more comfortable to remain in old habitual patterns, even if such patterns are neither healthy nor productive.

Even though there are predictable patterns—even seasons—of conflict, people can change. This is the hope that God's grace offers. We can learn new skills in addressing and responding to conflict each time it arises (rather than letting it go on and on unchecked), and in taking responsibility for collaboratively dealing with it. In the second part of this book we shall explore ways to respond to conflict that do not give power inappropriately to those who instigate, escalate, and even exploit conflict. We can develop new, positive patterns of moving through conflict and living a more fruitful life with one another and in ministry in the world.

Three Caveats on Resolution, Management, and Change

Healthy, Just Resolution

Some people believe conflict should be avoided or, if that is not possible, that it should be reduced, or resolved as quickly as possible. To resolve conflict in God's time is to claim the gift of reconciliation (not resignation) given by a gracious God in Jesus Christ. One could say that gift is the reality in which we live expectantly. It is a gift to be used—not an excuse for living any way we want. But because it is a gift, we do not need to grab any quick fix; we can trust this gracious, reconciling God to see us through even a long-term process of resolving conflict.

Sometimes conflict needs to escalate before healthy, just resolution is possible. When an oppressed group is locked in discrimination, to speak up, to caucus, to press forward toward their own liberation is necessary. To resolve the conflict too quickly would mean to return things to their original state, keeping the oppressed disadvantaged. But the more oppressed people continue to press on, the better chance that a more equitable partnership that is healthy for all can emerge. Those who gain from the status quo will continue to not recognize the issue. An example is what news media often refer to as a "race riot." Those who labor together toward freedom will name such a movement "rebellion." To wait for the oppressor group to want to deal with the issue of race would postpone engagement indefinitely.

This is not to negate the importance of resolving conflicts as soon as possible; it is to warn against one person or group using their power to stop the process before real change takes place. What are the conditions under which resolution is not only possible but also equitable? What are the signs that the time is right for genuine resolution? It is when communities, trusting a gracious God who has created, reconciled, and empowered people for healthy interdependence, give voice to all. It is when those in power lead wisely, relinquishing abusive power, and use their appropriate authority to guide a group toward healthy, equitable collaboration and resolution. [7] This is a vision of God's reign, and as such it is a worthy goal in dealing with conflict.

Management and Control

Specific instances of conflict need to be resolved in good time. But, knowing the human condition and being a student of history and organizations, one cannot assume that conflicts will ever be resolved to such an extent that no conflict will arise again. The goal of managing conflict is appropriate, if by that statement one does not mean managing people by keeping them under one's own control.

We might say that we intend not to control people but to control conflict, although even that goal may sometimes be beyond our power. None of us has the ability to totally control situations, any more than we can totally control people. We may assume things or people are under our control when there is no overt display of disagreement, but most of us realize that the conflict only goes underground. However, we can use our appropriate authority in our given roles to help create and maintain a safe, trustworthy environment in which people respect, listen to, communicate with, and work together to manage—and yes, resolve—their conflict. (In chapter 5 we shall discuss roles.) We can seek to manage ourselves (even that is not totally possible) through attention to our own responses to conflict, and through understanding our own histories with and images of conflict. As leaders we are called, not to abdicate, but to lead people and communities through conflict.

Conflict and Change

Some books and seminars equate reluctance to engage in conflict with inability to change. [8] Through direct or indirect examples, they label church institutions as inflexible, and that keeping a tradition is avoidance. Whereas being mired in the past is to fail to trust a living and leading God, following a cultural god is not necessarily better. The bright specter of "new and improved" can often lead people, not beyond conflict, but into a numbing fast-paced search for the latest, quickest, self-serving solution. Simply saying, "We have to move on" may liberate a group from being stuck. But a hasty moving on that negates rich history and disregards theological foundations will not position a congregation for faithful ministry.

Sometimes a change in leadership is called for to help a congregation claim its gifts and move beyond contention. However, habitual conflict will not be unlearned merely through a constant change of pastors. Change itself may become addictive, and simply changing pastors can be avoidance of conflict by a congregation. Congregations moving from contention to life-giving collaboration can trust a faithful God of history, of the present and of the unknown future, but they may need reminding.

Transformation

Short-term Objectives

When the path through conflict requires a long journey, having some short-term objectives is useful. Marriage counselors teach couples to engage in fair fights (although that term for a tactic is useful only if conflict is imaged as a "battle"). Workshop leaders teach listening skills to groups whose remarks seem to pass one another. Congregations also need skills of respect, empathy, challenge, and concern to address conflict.[9] When people cannot really hear one another, communication is impossible. Simply demanding that people collaborate won't work.

So, how can one develop short-term objectives? First, by understanding which direction a conflict is going. Does the conflict need to be contained rather than broadened? Is it destructive or productive? Here are some short-term strategies to help congregations set the stage for better communication:

- Agree to stop making accusations; listen to fears.
- Determine who needs to be involved in resolving this conflict.
- Discuss the type of conflict that exists (e.g., truth, values, mission, ministry).
- Provide opportunity to gather information about the issue.
- Set specific time guidelines for clarifying, debating, and brainstorming ideas.
- Begin to develop new skills for responding to conflict.
- Decide when and how the group will settle some matters and when to meet again to continue collaboration on broader issues.

Long-term Goals

Conflict is not static. It increases, diminishes, and changes. Although conflict may seem to have a life of its own, it need not be a mysterious process, or be allowed to become a force ready to demolish everything in its path. We can seek to understand the directions conflict takes and we can set realistic goals about the outcome of conflict. We can envision where we hope to be six weeks or six months or two years from now.

What goals do you have for your staff relationship? What goals do you have for yourself? What goals do you have for the church? If you are currently embroiled in a conflict, are you committed to working things through? Can you learn together how to listen to other visions for ministry? Can you set short-term objectives that are achievable so that you feel you are making progress on your journey toward a healthy way of living out your common mission?

Long-term goals are also important. People without a vision perish, so attention to these goals can provide consensus toward the church's overall direction and preempt some conflicts. Here are some long-term goals. They can be used as church goals, committee goals or, if there is a staff, staff goals:

- Commit as a group to developing healthy relationships that are able to deal with the stress of everyday life together.

- Pray together regularly and search the scriptures for ongoing growth. Make this a regular part of the meeting agenda.
- Celebrate ministries that have been happening. Give thanks to God and to one another often. Affirm the people who are contributing to collaborative ministry.
- Set regularly scheduled times to assess patterns of conflict in the congregation and to analyze directions they take. Be aware that there will be some resistance to doing this, so stress the importance of prevention.
- Note when healthy responses to conflict are used; reinforce positive skills. Use praise and affirmation; be genuine.
- Connect with needs and resources of other faith communities; gain perspective on your own situation through focusing on God's activity beyond your own church.
- Seek to be energized by one another's gifts and strengthened for sustained service, even in the midst of suffering. Serve one another as you would serve Christ.
- Constantly remind yourselves that Christ is the head of the church, including your own local congregation.

Personal Reflection

Take time for quiet reflection or write in a journal the story of two conflicts in your life journey. They may be recent or long ago. Recall the direction each took. Did they escalate? Were they habitual? Were there common elements in each or were they quite different? How do you deal with destructive and productive conflict? What would you like to learn about yourself through remembering these stories? What would you like others to know about how you handle conflict? What vision do you have for your church beyond any current conflicts?

Collegial Conversation

Begin with asking for God's guidance. Then look at the short-term objectives and long-term goals listed above. Using either a hypothetical or a current real-life conflict your faith community is facing, amend and extend those lists. Discuss roles you might play in that conflict and make some specific commitments to one another about collaborative efforts to address that conflict.

Notes

1. Joyce L. Hocker and William W. Wilmot, *Interpersonal Conflict*, 6th ed. (Boston: McGraw-Hill, 2001), pp. 48-62.
2. See chapter 5, "Roles in Conflict."
3. Speed Leas and Paul Kittlaus, *Church Fights* (Philadelphia: Westminster, 1973), pp. 41-42. Leas and Kittlaus wrote about conflict "gone awry." Although they laid the problem mostly on avoidance, they did acknowledge conflict that leads to violence and destruction. They contended those situations are rare. Thirty-some years later one can see destructive conflict is not so rare. Valid, however, is their point that it is *fear* of conflict going awry that disables, particularly when the perceived choices of response are either no engagement in conflict or all-out war.
4. Arthur Paul Boers, *Never Call Them Jerks: Healthy Responses to Difficult Behavior* (Bethesda, Md.: Alban, 1999), pp. 58-60, 66. Boers also quotes Edwin Friedman, Mansell Pattison, and Peter Steinke in pointing out that not only are retaliatory responses not helpful, but also nondirective, appeasing, or reasoning responses.
5. Marlin E. Thomas, ed., *Transforming Conflict in Your Church* (Scottdale, Pa.: Herald Press, 2002), pp. 29-33. Thomas writes about five levels of conflict: (1) problems to solve; (2) uncomfortable disagreement; (3) contest; (4) church fights; and (5) intractable contests. He stresses the importance of resolving the polarization of level three conflict before it reaches levels four and five of escalation.
6. Boers, *Never Call Them Jerks*, pp. 77-78. Boers notes that it is tempting to focus on those who behave irresponsibly, giving them too much power. He and other counselors emphasize that it is wise to work on those who are the healthiest, because they are often "overfunctioning" in response. Whereas that may be a quicker way of addressing the conflict in a counseling situation, such counselors may neglect to account for the toll it takes on the responsible, healthier members of a congregation.
7. Christine E. Iverson, "Ordinary Safety: Ministry in Conflict and Crisis" in Norma Cook Everist, ed., *Ordinary Ministry* (Nashville: Abingdon Press, 2000), pp. 160-66. Iverson likens ministry to a congregation in the crisis of conflict with disaster response ministry. She stresses providing clear boundaries to provide safety, laying a groundwork of policies to guide the congregation toward more healthy ways of

dealing with conflict, and describes how a congregation reached a turning point.

8. Many books are helpful for congregations dealing with or wanting to change. See, for example, Carl S. Dudley and Nancy T. Ammerman, *Congregations in Transition: A Guide for Analyzing, Assessing, and Adapting in Changing Communities* (San Francisco: Jossey-Bass, 2002), p. 11. The authors help congregations deal with the change, and possible conflict, which comes from communities changing. They help congregations move through transition by positive adaptation rather than resistance.

9. Ibid., pp. 65-67.

CHAPTER FOUR

PERSONAL HISTORY OF CONFLICT

C an you remember a time when you were quite young and you experienced or overheard people in conflict? Do you remember how it felt? Can you recall what you did? How we have handled conflict in the past influences how we are likely to respond to conflict in the present. Early memories of conflict in our family or at school can guide us in our understanding of ourselves and our responses.

Do you recall a congregational conflict that changed you? How did it change the congregation? Even though the human problem of contention, blame, alienation, and pain permeates every faith community, each congregation has faced conflict in its own unique way. Reflecting collaboratively on the corporate history of conflict can help people understand what happened, and give insights and skill for dealing with conflict in the present and the future. Although this chapter focuses on our own personal history with conflict, I want to emphasize how crucial listening to the stories of our congregations is to the people we serve. [1]

God of History, the Present, and the Future

Christianity is a historic faith, a living faith, and a faith that carries us and the whole church into the future. We confess we believe in a God who was, who is, and who is to come. God was faithful to the covenant God made with the Hebrew people. Throughout the Bible the people of God broke that covenant again and again, but God's unconditional love was steadfast. God remembered the promise and sent Jesus Christ to live amid the complexity of human conflict, and through the cross did not remember our sins against us, but put them to death that we might be liberated for new life.

We celebrate the gift of the church at Pentecost. Each time God's people gather to hear the Word of forgiveness and to partake of Holy Communion, we do this in remembrance of Christ. Throughout the history of the church, and throughout the world today in every congregation, human beings continue to forget God's unconditional love, but God is faithful, loving and liberating people to dwell in God's forgiveness even in the midst of conflict that may be tearing them apart. The history and presence of God's grace is worth remembering.

We confess we believe in a God who will continue to be faithful into the future. This redeeming and reconciling God continues to forgive, renew, and transform human lives in community. In the midst of the most wrenching conflict, we are called to live into God's promised future, trusting that God has already put together in perfect love that which we realize we will continue to break apart. No matter how real the alienation, nothing can separate us from the love of God in Christ Jesus. That gives hope, not in our own powers to live and work together, but in God's power to live in and through us in Jesus Christ. The God who was, who is, and who is to come is able to forgive and transform our own personal and communal histories and shape us for new life and new skill. Therefore, at this point in the book, we take time to reflect on our own personal histories.

Our History with Conflict

Who have we been in situations of conflict has shaped who we are today. This chapter is primarily about you, the reader, so early on you are invited to sit back, remember, and place your own history in these pages. [2]

Early Childhood

What is the earliest memory you have of conflict in your family? Was it loud? Subdued? Who was involved? Where were you? What was going on? How did you feel? What did you do? Do you have vivid recollections? Is it difficult to remember?

School Days

What do you recall about yourself at school? Picture yourself as a child in preschool, kindergarten, or early primary grades. What were you like? A leader? A follower? Did you get into trouble? Why? Were you a child who did what the teacher said most of the time? Why? Who were your friends?

Picture yourself at ten or eleven. What memories do you have from that time period, either of home or of school? Picture a time when you were involved in or witnessed conflict in those early school days. Where were you? What was going on? What did you say? What did you do? What did others around you do? What was the response of those in authority? How did you feel? After that day did you make any decisions about what you would do later? How do you feel about that memory now?

> *We cannot change our histories, but we can change the ways we interpret the past.*

Teenage Years

As you moved into your teenage years, what conflicts did

44

you experience inside yourself? At home? At school? With friends? What were you like at that age? How did you view conflict and how did you respond?

Recall some conflicted situation in which you had little power. What was that like? What patterns of response were you beginning to develop? How did you feel about yourself? How did you feel about your parents? Your friends? What did you do?

Picture a situation of conflict during your teenage years where you did have some power to determine the outcome. What role did you play? Remember how you felt about yourself and the world around you. Looking back, what strategies for dealing with conflict were you developing? What leadership skills in regard to conflict were emerging?

Adulthood

Think about where you lived, studied, and worked as a young adult. Was there some significant intrapersonal conflict that was part of the transition to young adulthood? How did you deal with that? Who helped you?

Recall one of the first work experiences you had as a young adult. What conflicts did you face? What were they about? Remember how you responded. What were you learning about dealing with conflict? What were you learning about yourself? What decisions were you making about living as an adult in a complex, diverse world?

In recent years, what have been some significant experiences you have had with conflict? Do you believe you are the same person you were a decade ago? How are you the same and how have you changed in regard to issues of conflict? Can you identify a time of transition when you feel you were changed or when you made a conscious decision to change the ways you dealt with conflict? Who helped you through that transition?

Who are you becoming? Experiences shape us for new insight. What has your own life experience taught you about conflict? What do you choose to learn from those experiences? What continued growth do you seek? What new skills in dealing with conflict do you plan to develop?

We cannot change our histories, but we can change the ways we interpret the past. Resting in the unconditional love of a God who is faithful through all the years of our lives, we can trust that we are forgiven and liberated from bondage to past pain. Living into God's promised future may be a gradual process, but we are empowered by the Spirit for transformation so that we can engage more productively in collaborative ministry and mission in a world that is burdened by destructive conflict.

Colleagues Reflect on Their Own Histories

Early Childhood

Francis: From my early childhood I can recall a tense feeling in the air because of unresolved differences. I have no vivid recollections of specific incidents that created that atmosphere in my home. But I do remember that conflict was not to be expressed or discussed among members of my family.

Eileen: I became aware through reflection that as a child I never felt either safe or free at home. Consequently, I spent my energy trying to be good so that things would be OK (typical of children of alcoholics) and doing things in secret.

School Days

Katie: In the third grade I suffered in silence when the boy who sat behind me started pulling out my hair. I thought perhaps the teacher might notice, but if she did, she did nothing to stop it. I didn't consider bringing it to her attention, nor did I say anything to my classmate. I don't believe I thought there was anything that I could do to change the situation. Sometimes outside of the classroom I would kick a boy who teased me, but I was not aggressive in the presence of adults. I was learning not to make waves, and to accept what I thought I couldn't change.

My strongest memories of conflict occurred about the age of nine or ten. It would be at night after I had gone to bed upstairs that I would hear my parents arguing downstairs. Actually, I remember hearing my father hollering followed by my mother crying. I felt afraid and worried that my parents might divorce. In the morning, I did not notice tension, but I also never saw my parents make up afterward. I never asked about what happened, nor did I even think of asking. Based on that experience I think that conflict has evoked vague but visceral feelings of fear throughout much of my life. I learned to be patient, to wait and see what would happen, and not to do anything that would increase conflict. I tried to do what was expected of me both at home and at school.

Ray: Conflict has taken a number of forms through my life. It has been gentle, loud, painful, scary, and something I have tried to control. As a child, conflict really scared me and I knew little about how to handle it.

I remember my teachers attempting to teach us how to deal with and manage conflict. There was the "count back from ten" method, the "just say no" method, and of course the cure-all method of seeking out an adult. None of these ever really worked for me. I would never deal with a conflict until it boiled up to the point where I would explode. I can remember four specific times when this happened. All of these explosions were at very stressful, new points in my life. In each, I ended up physically hurting another child. Because I have come to know that I am capable of doing harm, I have taken steps to monitor, or prevent, such conflicts from happening again.

I have discussed these events with pastors and a counselor. I know that I will never be free of conflict and that if I do not confront my anger I will once again release it in destructive ways.

Francis: I remember the days surrounding the Cuban missile crisis in the early 1960s and how frightened my folks seemed. I remember living in Chicago at the time and our public school instituted a public safety program. In case of nuclear attack we were trained to run home at the sound of the school bell. We were to indicate on a piece of paper the beginning time of our exit from school and my mom would have to fill out the part that indicated at what time I came through the door of our house. I think the school officials wanted to see how close some of us were to home so that they would know who could be released in case of an attack. This memory has created a lot of fear in me.

Teenage Years

Katie: I remember in my adolescent years that in order to compensate for the tense feelings, and in order to please my folks, I excelled at school. Academic achievement was a way for me to feel better about myself. I tried to stay in the background at school and usually stayed only with myself or a few close friends. When I was confronted with bullying from certain people, I usually avoided having to deal with actual fights by choosing to run rather than stand and fight. I came up with quite a catalog of avoidance techniques.[3]

Marie: Looking back, I realize I have been very accepting of others' opinions of who I am supposed to be in conflict and have most often accommodated others' views rather than stick up for my own. I remember in my adolescent years having conflicts with my parents and feeling like I wasn't being listened to or that my opinion didn't matter; I wasn't validated. From that point I tended to accommodate because my opinion wasn't important anyway, so why bother engaging in conflict.[4]

Adulthood

John: As I think back on my life, there are several incidents that have had a tremendous impact on my life and ministry. One was with a landlord. As a young adult I had been renting a furnished one-bedroom apartment. I needed to move to a larger place to accommodate my furniture, which I had been keeping at my parents' house. My parents were about to move. I found a small house and the owner was agreeable to letting me rent the house beginning the first of the upcoming month; he gave me the key.

I lined up friends to help move my belongings to short-term storage. I had a few houseplants and I decided to drop them off at the rental house early in the morning before work. The landlord couple lived next door and stormed over in their pajamas angrily accusing me of sneaking in for a couple weeks of free rent. I explained to them that I was merely dropping off a few plants, was not moving in, and agreed to not even set foot there again until the official rental period began.

I generally had no contact with my landlord or his family over the two years I was there. However, the few contacts I did have were most often confrontational. I kept my composure even when it was evident that the landlord was looking for a physical fight. My calm manner diffused the potentially volatile situation without any blows. I had learned the hard way in junior and senior high school that fighting was a stupid way of handling disagreements and conflict.

I decided to move out two summers later. A couple of years after that I read in the paper about a subsequent altercation that the landlord had had with his business associate, which had put the associate in the hospital and the landlord in jail on assault and battery charges. So I count my blessings for not being goaded into a fistfight. I rely heavily upon my experiences with those encounters to maintain a relaxed posture and voice when I am faced with similar situations.

Annika: In reflecting on stories from my childhood, now as an adult I see my particular tendency to allow a conflict to consume me. When I'm almost at that state, I run away in an attempt at self-preservation. Then I question myself. Was I at fault? Maybe my running is an admission of guilt. Maybe I'm afraid of losing the comfort of community. How unhelpful that feeling is in resolving conflict! [5]

Significant Learnings in Recent Years

Marie: In recent years, I have made a decision to make changes in how I handle conflict. I am beginning to find my voice and know that my opinion is just as valid as everyone else's. I try to focus on what others have to say and what lies behind their words. Rather than walking away from conflict or always being accommodating, I try to stay involved in the process of working through the conflict.

Annika: I am making some drastic shifts in how I choose to deal with conflict, too. I believe that conflict in its most destructive forms devours the most vulnerable first. In this game there are two unhealthy positions: the martyr and the destroyer. Neither role is necessary in collaborative conflict. No one needs to feed or be fed on the pain of others. Neither should anyone feel the need to sacrifice his or her well-being or conscience on the altar of appeasement. Christ's work is already done.

Katie: I recognize that when people are under stress they may lash out but caregivers (and empathetic listeners) need not take it personally. It is important to provide a safe space for hurting people to express their deep feelings without being judged. I have been learning to express my opinions, too, without being afraid of backlash when I differ with people. I am learning to confine a critical incident, giving it no larger space than it deserves. This helps me in being able to accept constructive criticism without feeling wounded. I don't expect that I will ever seek out conflict, but now I trust my judgment, ask questions that help clarify my perceptions, and have achieved a level of differentiation that helps me distinguish between issues and relationships in the midst of conflict.

Today

Think of three different roles in your life today (e.g., pastor, parent, community social service board member). When there is conflict in that place (institution, relationship, and so forth), how are you likely to respond? What skills and understandings do you now possess to help you deal with conflict there?

Remembering Congregational Conflict

Most of this chapter has been about our personal history with conflict. It is important we do not shortchange reflection upon such personal histories. Our intrapersonal conflict and our history of interpersonal conflict shape the images we have of conflict and influence the roles we play in congregational conflict.

This entire book is about conflict in the congregation, and we will continue to examine roles and responses to conflict in the remainder of the book. However, at this point, briefly, we do well to think about our history with conflict in communities of faith.

Remember

What are your first memories of being part of a faith community? What was the atmosphere in the congregation that shaped your faith formation? What conflicts in the church (local, regional, or national) have you been part of or witnessed? Did they surprise you, worry you, distress you? Who was involved? Was the conflict interpersonal? Was it over truth (facts), beliefs (issues), worth (values), mission (goals), or ministry (means)? What was at stake?

What happened? What role(s) did you play? What was the outcome? How did that shape your feelings about the church? What decisions did you make as a result?

Katie: When I was a junior in high school there was conflict in my church. I don't know what it was about, but the congregation asked my pastor to leave. He was the second of three who experienced the same treatment. I remember him pleading from the pulpit to be allowed to stay until his daughter, who was a senior at the time, could finish high school. It was not to be; she came to live with our family. Through that experience I developed compassion for people who are victims of a situation or system beyond their control.

Katie as a young girl experienced church conflict from the perspective of being part of the family of caring laity. Some of us have been that pastor who was asked to leave. Some of us have had to ask for the resignation of a staff member. Some of us have been in the very difficult position of being the spouse of a leader wounded in a church fight. Some of us have lived through a major church schism. Perhaps we have led a movement for a change that we knew would cause conflict. At the time, we desperately hoped the effort would be productive and not destructive. Memories of such histories can be overwhelming unless and until we remember the covenant faithfulness of a God who enters human experience and human conflict. People of faith have a long history of harming their own prophets and hurting their own saints. Pastors are often wounded healers, those wounds being inflicted by their own churches. We are called to love God's people, but not to become a scapegoat or sacrifice. Christ has already laid down his life for the church. This forgiving, reconciling God can heal memories and give new life so that, no matter how difficult, we can continue to collaborate, to work together, in God's indispensable church. [6]

Personal Reflection

During your remembering in this chapter you may have uncovered some particularly significant events in your life that deserve further, deeper, reflection. Schedule some time with a significant person in your life, such as a mentor, spiritual guide, or counselor to explore further some of these things. In addition, you might wish to use prayer, guided meditation, or journal writing.

Collegial Conversation

Collegial conversation is an important element to sustain productive ministry, but it can be tricky. Today's colleague may be tomorrow's regional minister or district superintendent, and you may worry about that. However, having said that, consider taking some time to have a collegial conversation about your history with conflict. Realize that talking about past conflict can be very unsettling for you and other people. Depending upon how comfortable your colleagues are and how much is at stake right now, you will need to discern how, when, and where (perhaps a retreat center) to have such a conversation. You may benefit from the guidance of a professional in this process. We are all tempted to think when things are going that well we can postpone such a conversation. However, it may be during the absence of crises that we will have the objectivity to gain from such work—and it is work.

Notes

1. Craig L. Nessan, *Beyond Maintenance to Mission: A Theology of the Congregation* (Minneapolis: Fortress Press, 1999), pp. 13-23.

2. Joyce L. Hocker and William W. Wilmot, *Interpersonal Conflict*, 6th ed. (Boston: McGraw-Hill, 2002), pp. 6-16.

3. James D. Whitehead and Evelyn Eaton Whitehead, *The Promise of Partnership: A Model for Collaborative Ministry* (San Francisco: HarperSanFrancisco, 1991), pp. 27-48. The Whiteheads help the reader deal with "the wounds of authority" and face the "shadows on the journey," particularly the shadow of conflict (pp. 40-41).

4. Evelyn Eaton Whitehead and James D. Whitehead, *Community of Faith: Crafting Christian Communities Today* (Mystic, Conn.: Twenty-third Publications, 1992), pp. 140-49. "Indifference is a greater enemy of community than is conflict" (p. 145).

5. See Katie Day, *Difficult Conversations: Taking Risks, Acting with Integrity* (Bethesda, Md.: Alban, 2001), pp. 13-16.

6. Norma Cook Everist, ed., *The Difficult But Indispensable Church* (Minneapolis, Fortress Press, 2002).

CHAPTER FIVE

ROLES IN CONFLICT

Pick your battles!" the young pastor was advised.
"Pick your role!" I would say in response. "Discern carefully the role you can play and cannot play. When you have a choice, select with wisdom the appropriate role to play and carry it through with skill."

So, how do you know what roles are available? How do you figure out what is going on so that you know where you should be involved? Our own personal histories with conflict contribute to the roles we play. How can you have enough perspective to discern when you are not the best person to be a mediator but instead need to draw on the skill of someone outside the fray? How can a pastor retain pastoral authority and yet step aside and let someone else lead in the midst of conflict?

And even when you clearly establish that you do have a contribution to make, what skills will you need in a particular kind of conflict? For a pastor, when is it best to be a teacher, guide, counselor, or priest? How does a pastor discern which is most effective when?

Outcomes and Relationships

Is it worth it? That's probably a phrase that should come after the advice, "Pick your battles." First of all, the reader will note that "battle" is just one of the many images of conflict, as explored in chapter 1. In any event, one always needs to consider the importance of outcomes and relationships. [1] For example, I might choose to play a strong leadership role of theologian if confessional *truths* are so much at stake that I truly believe the church would no longer be the church if doctrines were compromised. The *outcome* is extremely important. Even when the issue is intrapersonal or interpersonal, the *outcome* may be at stake if people are acting in such a destructive way that the *mission* of the church is impaired.

On the other side of the scale, one may not want to engage in "battle" or compete to win an argument or choose the role of taking control if the *outcome* is less important than the *relationship*. [2] If I want a group to move through a conflict with relationships in tact, I will utilize a different response. For example, I may choose the response of accommodation if a difference arises over whose car the visitation team will use to visit the local care center. [3] How we get there is less important than that we go together.

Determining the relative importance of outcomes and relationships in a given situation at a given time is one factor in determining what roles leaders should or should not play. Choosing how much energy to invest in a conflict is only a small part of a collaborative approach to conflict. We have a variety of roles and responses available to us as leaders of faith communities. In this chapter we shall explore roles, and have some fun thinking through some role-playing options. But first it is important to remember that we are called to be leaders in faith communities; we are not God.

Remembering Who Is and Who Is Not God

When struggling to control conflict, the bad news is: I am not God. I cannot control my congregation members, for they do not belong to me. [4] I cannot take care of the people I serve in such a way that they will never hurt one another. I cannot determine people's feelings or actions. I cannot play God for I am not God, and pretending I am will lead only to frustration on my part and disappointment, anger, or dependency on the part of people among whom I minister. [5]

Realizing this, however, we also need to remember that the good news is: I am not God. God is God, and therefore I am liberated from the pretentious posture of either wanting or feeling I need to be. The Creator God continues to create new possibilities, new resources, and that wonderful gift of time. Most of all, I need to remember that God is a God of steadfast love and faithfulness and will not forsake God's people even amid our unfaithfulness to one another. Now, if only the congregation would stop expecting miracles from me.

Jesus the Christ was born into a world of conflict. There is no conflict that is beyond what Jesus has already encountered. He was the object of ridicule, abuse, and suffering. Therefore, when I suffer—and I will—because of contentious conflict in the congregation, I can remember that I can release this suffering into the hands of the Suffering Servant. When I am the object of scorn, and even when I am unjustly accused, I need to remember I am not called to be martyr, savior, or sacrificial lamb. Christ's sacrifice is complete. The Resurrection is real and new life through believing in the forgiveness of sins is not only possible but a reality. My identity is not in my role (e.g., leader, pastor, mediator, care giver). Through my baptism, Christ has given me a new identity as God's forgiven child and frees me to assume an appropriate role as needed for service in Christ's name. I may suffer, but no one can ultimately destroy my relation to God in Christ Jesus.

When it seems difficult to believe that our congregation will make it through the dark days of destructive conflict, the Holy Spirit can breathe into our spirit—belief in God being God, redeeming the worst of scenarios and recreating community. This may not come immediately; it will take time—God's time. Nor will God remove from our midst people we think are the troublemakers. (That is wanting to play God, determining who is or who is not part of the Body of Christ.) But we also need to remember that when people in the congregation try to control the agenda with their own negativity, we as leaders in this community of faith are called to not allow *them* to assume the role of God. They are not God. I am not God. But God *is* God, continuing to protect, provide, create, redeem, forgive, restore, and transform God's people sometimes in spite of the church.

For Reflection
1. Think of a time of conflict in your congregation when a person tried to take God's role of judgment. Think of a time when someone inappropriately claimed power by disrupting the agenda and steering a conflict in a direction that benefited only that one person. What happened to the group? How might it have gone differently?
2. What are your own propensities to assume the role of God? Under the stress of conflict, are you more likely to think you are omniscient (knowing people's minds and motives)? Omnipotent (able to control the situation)? Omnipresent (able to be everywhere at once taking care of everyone)? How might you relinquish the pretense? Who is most effective in reminding you that you are not God?

Types of Conflict and Appropriate Roles

Intrapersonal and Interpersonal Conflict

When conflict is my own intrapersonal conflict, my role will not be to become theologian, or priest, or prophet. Pastors sometimes say they preach to themselves, and whereas pastoral ministers need to search the scriptures daily, the Bible does not show us leaders preaching to themselves. Within the Body of Christ we need not and cannot be our own prophet or priest. That is a time when we need the counsel of some else. That is a time to seek out a person who can be priest and guide to us.

Many leaders of religious communities have great skill,

> *We are so used to the role of facilitating reconciliation that we may be slow to see when the conflict involves us or is about us.*

compassion, and patience in serving as counselor, mediator, and priest for people or groups of people in the midst of interpersonal conflict. That role is an important part of ministry. However, when the pastor is one of the parties in the interpersonal conflict, he or she cannot play the role of mediator in *that* situation. Pastors often make that mistake. We are so used to the role of being the one to facilitate reconciliation that we may be slow to see when the interpersonal conflict involves us, or when the issue is *about* us. In this particular conflict we will need someone other than ourselves from the broader church to serve in that role. [6]

Conflict over Issues, Truth, Values, Goals, or Means

When it is clear that the current conflict is not primarily an intrapersonal or an interpersonal struggle (although, as we have seen, our own issues and person are never totally out of the picture), we still need to figure out which particular leadership role is necessary according to the kind of conflict.

If the conflict is over beliefs (issues), we may be called to the role of theologian or priest. If the conflict is over truth (facts), we may be called to the role of teacher. If the conflict is over worth (values), we may be called to the role of pastoral counselor. If the conflict is over mission (goals), we may be called to the role of prophet. If the conflict is over ministry (means), we may be called to the role of visionary leader.

But even this is too simple; for within the roles we may wish to play the complexity of the situation and the community's ever changing needs call for even more careful discernment. If the community is in pain, their nerves raw and their tears fresh, they will need care, compassion, and a listening, validating, but not judging ear. If the community has lost perspective, is distorting facts and hurling accusations at one another, they will need time to back off, to calm down, to take a fresh look at the issues and at one another. If the conflict is spreading, with more and more people being implicated, and if the issues are being exaggerated, the need is for someone to say, "Stop!" and to draw boundaries. If the community has inflicted harm upon one another, or refused to carry out their mission, their need is for repentance, confession, and absolution. If the community needs to move beyond stagnation, complaint, and excuse, their need is for vision.

What skills will the leader need? What insight? What courage?

Two Role-plays

Role-plays can be fun. They also provide opportunity to nuance issues and for people to discover their own feelings experientially. Role-plays can also be powerful, so you will need to debrief afterward. Two role-plays follow. They can be used with a church staff, council, committee, or colleague group. The group would do well to select a fictitious situation. (If a group wants to use role-play during an actual conflict they will need a skilled person from outside the group to guide the role-play and discussion.)

As a leader, invite people to take the various parts. Depending upon the size of the group, some may be observers. Let the role-play go on for a few minutes, stopping it when it seems enough has happened for fruitful discussion. Give at least twice the amount of time for debriefing. Ask the actors themselves the debriefing questions first. Then ask any observers what they saw and heard. The aim of role-play is not to make a point, but open-ended learning.

Role-play 1: The scene is a faith community (congregation, outdoor or campus ministry, and so forth) where a conflict is *new.*

Invite the actors to spontaneously make up the nature of the conflict. Emotions are raw and people are tense.

Enter: a minister choosing to be "teacher" in this situation.

Debrief: What happened or did not happen? How did people feel? What was said? What was left unsaid but thought?

Now play the scene again, beginning the same way.

Enter: a minister assuming the role of "pastoral counselor."

Debrief: What happened? How did people feel? What changes took place? What was said? What was still beneath the surface?

Role-play 2: The scene is a faith community where the conflict has been going on for some time and is now escalating to the point of getting out of hand. It is also widening. More and more people are being drawn in. The initial issues have multiplied. Once again, invite the actors to make up the conflict.

Enter: a minister assuming the role of "pastoral counselor."

Debrief: What happened? What did not happen? Who said what? What happened next? What did people feel? Which direction were emotions going?

Now play the scene again beginning the same way.

Enter: a minister assuming the role of a leader with vision.

Debrief: What happened immediately? How did people feel? What happened next? What was said and by whom? What direction did the emotions go?

Role-plays help us gain insight experientially. They help a group understand what may be going on beneath the surface in complex relationships. They also provide opportunity to "try on" different roles and approaches.

The Opportunities in Role Clarity

Role clarity is helpful. But we will not be equally skilled or comfortable in each of the roles. For some ministerial leaders the role of pastoral counselor—being supportive of everyone involved in the conflict—is most familiar, whereas the role of prophet is less so. For others the role of visionary leader—setting clear boundaries for dealing with conflict, helping focus the group on the future—is the preferred approach, whereas the role of confessor and priest is less comfortable. Growing more aware, differentiating the self, gaining more skills and more confidence in a variety of roles (and in a variety of *responses* to conflict, which we deal with in the second part of this book), provides options and helps us be appropriately active rather than merely reactive or defensive. [7]

Integrity and Authenticity

Still, the reader may feel that the concept of discerning and playing different roles is artificial or superficial. Ministerial leaders may fear they will be seen as inauthentic or even shifty. The word *role* may imply merely acting a part. This is not the goal. Artificially acting a role may signal internal confusion (intrapersonal conflict about the nature of the conflict), or avoidance of genuine engagement. None of us wants that.

Clarifying the type of leadership needed is a way to genuinely meet the community where they are while at all times responsibly exercising the authority of our office. [8] Such discernment will take careful listening and observation, prayer, and counsel. [9] The process of role selection is not a case of deception but of seeking the truth and being authentic. Too often we allow external circumstances to dictate our role and we play out the expected or the familiar one. Selecting the role one plays within a conflict is an important choice to exercise.

One pastor told of a time early in his ministry in a congregation when the council president came into the pastor's office to ask what he was going to do about "that Jones family." The pastor listened with care and compassion for a while to stories of conflict and hurt that had been going on for years. Then there came a time in the conversation when the pastor's role changed from that of caring listener to the role of prophet and confronter: "What would you have me *do* with them?" he asked. "I am called to be their pastor just as much as I am called to be yours!"

That was a critical point of discernment for the new pastor in his many roles in that congregation. If he had maintained only the role of caring listener or had abdicated his role of pastor to the entire congregation in simply going along with the council president's agenda, he would have lost credibility as an effective leader with a significant percentage of the congregation. In the coming months his role had to change a number of times, sometimes with the very same people, over the very same issues, depending upon the particular events in the ongoing conflict and the needs of the people involved.

Reception of Roles

One must also consider what role the community will receive and how they in turn will alter the role with their own responses. One cannot merely claim a role and enact it. The roles that individuals can choose to play in conflict are partially defined by the receptivity of others within the conflict. Role clarity, however, can help us be clear inside ourselves and in our leadership. Then we will be less likely to be goaded into giving only support when we need to provide a prophetic voice about mission. When we take time to observe, listen, and pray, people may be more open to receiving not just what they thought they wanted—"a dynamic leader who will put a stop to the argument"—but a person who chooses to set up opportunities for all voices to be heard so that the community can pursue truth. When people learn that we are capable of more than one ministerial response, they become more able to receive and interact accordingly.

In conflict over issues and facts, ministerial leaders often wonder about the rightness or wrongness of offering their personal opinion in the midst of conflict. When the outcome is less important than the relationship, we may easily be able to spend our energy setting a trustworthy environment, guiding the conversation, and making sure all voices are heard. But when we have a personal stake in the issue, it is more difficult to separate our role as leader *of* the group discussion from being an individual with a point of view we want to express *in* that discussion.

Even when we don't have a particular opinion, congregation members may assume we do. (Maybe they are right; maybe we are simply kidding ourselves in believing we are neutral.) In either case, role clarity and communicating the role we are playing on this occasion is very important. When we have a definite opinion, we might ask someone else to serve as the one who leads and maintains a trustworthy environment, either for the entire session or for that portion of the meeting. Even if we have carefully done that and then expressed our opinion, when one is still leader of the community people will carry our personal view in a conflict over into our other relationships with them. Being honest about our views, particularly about when we need to exercise an authoritative opinion, is important. Then we will also need to faithfully carry out our responsibilities in the rest of our ministry in ways that demonstrate our care for each member of the community.

The Varied Roles and Gifts of All

The ministerial leader is not the only person who can gain from role clarity. Congregational leaders becoming more familiar with the different roles needed in a conflicted situation and being aware of their own favorite roles can also open the congregation to understanding and developing skill in a variety of responses to conflict. [10] We need a range of diverse ideas in a congregation. In the midst of conflict we also need different people playing different roles, purposefully, not just randomly. [11] During a division over facts, some people can be commissioned to become fact finders. When a troubled and troubling person's intrapersonal conflict spills over into the congregation's building program, a congregation member not on the building committee might be able to be a caregiver without being triangulated into the conflict. Such sharing of roles can help the congregation deal more creatively and collaboratively with conflict. [12]

Personal Reflection and Collegial Conversation
Below are several questions. Question 1 is a good place to begin personal reflection. Questions 2 and 3 would be helpful for

a collegial conversation. Question 4 helps us consider roles beyond the congregation, both individually and as a faith community. Use these questions as appropriate to your situation. For example, although question 1 is very personal, sharing conversation about it with a trusted colleague could be very useful. Likewise, although question 3 relates directly to a faith community, doing some thoughtful, honest reflection will help prepare for collegial conversation.

1. Am I conflicted within?

   - Am I tired? Sick? Lonely? Bored? Angry? Stressed? Depressed? Spiritually drained? [13]
   - Do I have a vocational conflict?
   - Do I have some unresolved grief, anger, or bitterness?
   - What else is going on in my life right now?
   - In a congregational conflict I might be able to play the role of_____.
   - At this time I cannot play the role of _____.
   - I could seek help from_____.

2. Is the conflict *about* me or does it involve me personally?

   - Am I the issue (e.g., the effectiveness of my ministry)?
   - Am I emotionally involved in the issue to the point of not being able to be objective?
   - Is the conflict interpersonal, between me and another person (or group of people)?
   - What role can I not play?
   - What role can another person play? Who? (And who not?)
   - Who from outside might be able to mediate this conflict?

3. Is the conflict over an issue, a goal, or means toward a goal?

   - Do I have a strong opinion?
   - Am I really able to be neutral?
   - Do I have a hidden opinion or agenda?
   - How high are the stakes?
   - How high is the stress on the relationships in the group?
   - What is the history of conflict here?
   - What role do I play if I have an opinion?

- What role do I play if I genuinely am neutral?
- How do I set a trustworthy environment for people to deal with the conflict?
- What additional roles might I play in the community during this stressful time? If I cannot, who else could?

4. What conflict in my community, state, nation, or world troubles me?

- What role do I play as a citizen?
- What role do I play as leader in my faith community?
- How public do I, or can I, make my position on an issue in the community?
- How able are parishioners to distinguish my role as citizen from my ecclesial role?
- Should I take a public stand? How should I decide?
- With whom might I consult about taking a public stand?
- What role would I like to play? At what cost?
- What role should I not play? At what cost?
- What roles are other people playing?
- How can I discern my long-term role in this conflict?

The question of role will always raise questions. Being able to choose the appropriate role to play in a given conflict requires understanding and gaining the skill of determining a variety of responses to conflict. We shall address seven such responses in the second part of this book.

Notes

1. Celia Allison Hahn, *Growing in Authority, Relinquishing Control* (Bethesda, Md.: Alban, 1994), pp. 43-52. Hahn provides helpful insights on being "people-oriented" and "task-oriented."
2. Chapters 8 and 9 in this book deal with the responses to conflict of "competition" and "control."
3. Chapter 10 in this book deals with the response of "accommodation."
4. Even though we are not omnipotent and cannot control people, "control" is a response to conflict that we shall examine, both positively and negatively, in chapter 9.
5. Otto F. Kernberg, *Ideology, Conflict and Leadership in Groups and Organizations* (New Haven, Conn.: Yale University Press, 1998), pp. 140-55. Kernberg describes the leader who needs to be in complete control.

6. An obvious choice is one's district superintendent, bishop, or presbyter. Given the working polity, it is wise to mutually discern if this is the appropriate choice because here, too, there may be a confusion of roles if that person has authority in other ways in the situation. The person to call in may be one designated by the judicatory leader, or a counselor who serves pastors and congregations in the area.

7. Arthur Paul Boers, *Never Call Them Jerks: Healthy Responses to Difficult Behavior* (Bethesda, Md.: Alban, 1999), pp. 92-107. Boers stresses the importance of differentiation in taking a nonreactive stance. Differentiation does not mean being cut off, but staying in touch in healthy ways (p. 98).

8. See Jackson W. Carroll, *As One with Authority* (Louisville: Westminster John Knox, 1991).

9. Ronald W. Richardson, *Creating a Healthier Church* (Minneapolis: Fortress Press, 1996), pp. 92-51, 172-83. Richardson writes about the *less* anxious presence (for none of us can be totally nonanxious), self-differentiation, and objectivity. By authentically seeking to understand, one can change the atmosphere. It may take the group some time to adjust to the leader's differentiation.

10. James D. Whitehead and Evelyn Eaton Whitehead, *The Promise of Partnership* (San Francisco: HarperSanFrancisco, 1991), pp. 131-32. The Whiteheads describe two styles of leadership, the first portraying the leader as powerful and the congregation as weak. The "leader prays and heals in ways the rest of us cannot" (p. 131). In the second style, the leader invites others to step forward rather than to step back. Whether at a bedside or in the midst of conflict, "the leader generates and guides this symbolic action of a community instead of simply supplying it" (p. 132).

11. Hugh F. Halverstadt, *Managing Church Conflict* (Louisville: Westminster John Knox, 1991), pp. 44-56, 133-48. Halverstadt defines roles in conflictive situations as "Principles," "Bystanders," "Third Parties," and "Arbiters." It is important to distinguish roles, although a person may play more than one. For example, bystanders can serve as coaches in nonadversarial ways. There are times when a principal needs to secure "coaching" for himself or herself.

12. See William Ury, *Getting to Peace* (New York: Viking Press, 1999). Ury's premise is that there is a role for "the third side." A community can prevent conflict by being provider, teacher, bridge builder; they can resolve conflict by being mediator, arbiter, equalizer, healer; they can contain a conflict by being witness, referee, and peacekeeper (p. vii).

13. Marshall Shelley, ed., *Leading Your Church Through Conflict and Reconciliation* (Minneapolis: Bethany, 1997), pp. 17-37. The authors use the term "high-voltage pain" and write of the necessity of rest.

PART 2

Responses to Conflict

AVOIDANCE

S urely I'm a coward when it comes to conflict. I like to avoid it!"
Such self-disclosure is accompanied with apology and frequently a call for help. We know conflict cannot be avoided, at least not forever, and not completely. But sometimes to avoid conflict is not altogether bad. [1] At times avoidance is exactly the right strategy. When the time is not right or the circumstances too volatile, it is a wise person who selects avoidance as the appropriate response.

To deny that conflict does not or should not exist is one thing. To choose avoidance as a *style* of response is quite another. [2] Avoidance may be a strong leadership style in a given atmosphere. Whereas a person may think himself or herself courageous in *confronting* a situation head-on, battering one's way through may be the weak way out. Being patient with people and taking time to gather information takes internal fortitude. [3]

> *Whether our choice to avoid conflict is negative or positive, we have made a choice.*

To avoid the very thought of conflict, however, is problematic. We need to look at our personal histories. What are our fears? What are our doubts? What are the skills we think we lack to engage conflict when necessary? Becoming more aware will free us from unhealthy avoidance and strengthen our skill to choose and use avoidance when it is the best response in a particular situation.

Avoidance in the Ministry of Jesus

How often have we heard the story of Jesus' overturning the tables in the Temple quoted to prove the Messiah got angry? Some people who quote Mark 11:15, Matthew 21:12, Luke 19:45, or John 2:13-16 (Luke doesn't even have Jesus overturning the tables) may be doing so to justify their own tempers. But have we noticed the times when Jesus avoided contention?[4]

- Jesus avoided a public encounter because his time had not yet come (John 7:1-13).
- Jesus refused to argue *about* Sabbath laws. He silenced their accusations with a question and then he healed a person in need (Luke 14:1-6).
- Jesus avoided conflict when synagogue leaders, filled with rage, wanted to hurl him off a cliff. "He passed through the midst of them and went on his way" (Luke 4:28-30).
- Jesus avoided judging people and sometimes purposely changed the subject to broaden their perspective (for example, Luke 7:36-50).
- Jesus avoided (ignored) the disciples' admonition to parents to keep their children away from him. He was direct: "Let the little children come to me, and do not stop them" (Luke 18:15-16).
- On one occasion Jesus avoided his mother and brothers (Luke 8:19-21). Should we interpret this to mean he couldn't face his family-of-origin issues? Or was this specific avoidance for the sake of his larger mission, to include a larger companionship? "My mother and my brothers are those who hear the word of God and do it" (Luke 8:21).
- When a conflict arose over lack of resources, Jesus avoided feeding the crowds, not because he did not care, or because

he could not face the crowds, but to involve his disciples in the ministry of feeding. When his disciples saw only scarcity, Jesus blessed and broke the loaves and "gave them to the disciples to set before the crowd" (Luke 9:12-17).

- Jesus avoided the conflict of notoriety (for example, Luke 9:21). "He sternly ordered and commanded [the disciples] not to tell anyone."
- Jesus avoided even those who were ready to receive him (Luke 9:51-56) because "he set his face to go to Jerusalem" (v. 51).
- Jesus did not avoid the cross. In avoiding reacting violently, even when faced with death, he was actively seeking a new way of living in the reign of God. Redemptive violence is a myth. Through the cross and resurrection God brings reconciliation and new life.

Images and History and Uses of Avoidance

We experience and use avoidance every day. Because conflict is part of daily life, to constantly engage in combat would consume us. However, to avoid every difficult situation would produce a life devoid of any possibility for fruitful collaboration. Once again it is helpful to examine our own images of conflict and to reflect on our own histories with conflict—in this case, avoidance. Then we will be better prepared to explore negative and positive uses of avoidance.

Images of Avoidance

How do you image avoidance? A cat circumventing a puddle? A child hiding under the table? An older adult sitting quietly watching middle-agers entangle themselves in disagreement? One man painted the word picture of "fallen leaves in a gently flowing stream naturally avoiding hitting rocks protruding from the stream bed."

How do we image persons who avoid conflict? Are they quiet? A person may appear to be wisely patient or gentle, and peace-loving but actually inside be full of built-up anger and frustration. [5] Is he or she strongly verbal and adept with language? A person may use language either to manipulatively divert, or to astutely respectfully guide a group through a timely engagement with conflict.

For Reflection

1. Think of one negative and one positive image of avoidance. What aspects of each response to conflict do these images bring up for you?
2. Think about people who use avoidance in wise, helpful ways. How do they do this? What do they say? What do you notice about their leadership style?

Our History of Avoidance

When we were younger, lacked power over our own lives, and had limited experience in dealing with complex situations, we may have adopted some avoidance strategies that we then needed. Samantha had a strategy of using her older sister to deal with her parents when they were particularly demanding. Samantha thought her voice too small, too unconvincing. Paul, having had one encounter with two boys who bullied him on the way to school, began leaving for school fifteen minutes early and went three blocks out of his way to avoid the boys. Such avoidance strategies are formative. Paul and Samantha may have broadened their range of responses to conflict as they grew up, or they may have found that they continued to respond to conflict with the same patterns of avoidance established in childhood.

Young adults develop strategies at the workplace to avoid conflict with the boss or to avoid becoming embroiled in office politics. Such strategies may provide helpful tools for lifelong patterns of seeking clarity on when to engage conflict and when to wisely discern "that is not my place." Or strategies of avoidance may stunt our growth. We need engagement with people whose ideas challenge our own. How do we know the difference? How can we know which strategies to drop and which skills to develop and when to use them?

The Hutchinson family experienced great disappointment with their congregation because of continuing conflict. They avoided the issues by joining another church. There, they were unhappily surprised to find different but equally disturbing conflict. Once again they began looking for a new congregation in which to worship.

Kathy Peterson served on a staff of a large congregation as a youth leader. She managed to avoid being "eaten up" by conflict, as she imaged it, by avoiding collaborating with what she perceived to be powerful chair people of influential committees and with the senior pastor. But now she is beginning a new position in a church in another part of the country. Will she carry her avoidance with her into her new ministerial leadership role?

For Reflection

1. Recall some specific ways that you as a child avoided being hurt by conflict. (Not all children have been able to avoid such pain.) How did it work for you? Are there some ways in which you still use those strategies? With whom? In what ways are they helpful now? In what ways are they not helpful?

2. As a young person going off to a college or a first job, what were some new encounters with conflict that were unfamiliar to you in your family of origin? How did you choose to avoid or not avoid conflict? Have you made some changes in your use of avoidance since then?

3. As a member of a congregation or as a ministerial leader, how have you seen avoidance used? Recall a situation in which avoidance delayed fruitful engagement. Recall a situation when an avoidance response helped prevent unhealthy escalation of a conflict.

Negative and Positive Uses of Avoidance

Negative Uses of Avoidance

- As a means of continual denial
- As a means not to value certain people
- As a way to think the conflict will just go away
- As a passive aggressive move to get what we want
- As a power play to make decisions unilaterally
- As a way not to admit we were wrong
- As a way to not have to claim our own authority
- As a way to maintain our belief that nothing can, or should, change
- As a way to get out of a situation, leaving someone else to clean up our mess

Phrases That Display Unhealthy Avoidance

"I don't see why I have to deal with that!"
"You're always a troublemaker. I'm leaving."
"The church should be a place of peace and tranquillity. Why do we have to fight?"
"Let's talk about something else."[6]
"That's ridiculous (laughter)."
"Why do you always have to make a mountain out of a molehill?"
"Whatever! I don't care anymore."

Positive Uses of Avoidance

- Providing reasonable time to gather necessary information
- Clarifying the issues and gaining some perspective
- Inviting the necessary parties to be present

- Regaining composure
- Securing the safety of others and self
- Preserving fragile unity and allowing time to strengthen the group
- Conserving energy that might be expended needlessly
- Devoting energy to other conflicts that are more important (although one "insignificant" issue may be masking a deeper issue) [7]
- Providing a quieting-down time so that people are not reactive but thoughtfully prepared to deal with the conflict

Phrases for Healthy Use of Avoidance Response

"I'm too emotionally tired to have this conversation right now, but I do want to deal with it because I value our relationship."

"I would rather we talk about this at another time. Are you free tomorrow morning (evening)? Would seven o'clock be OK? We could meet at . . ."

"I realize not all of us can express what we think or feel about this issue right now."

"It appears that some of us may have undue influence in this difficult decision. We need to provide everyone with all the facts."

(Depending on your image of conflict) "Let's sleep on it." "Let's mull it over." "Let's let the dust settle on this one."

"You bring up a good point. We need to bring others into this discussion."

Listening in on a Conversation About Avoidance

People use avoidance as a response to conflict in different ways. In the following conversation, listen for the images of conflict and for openness to growth.

Jessie: Sometimes it's good not to put gasoline on the fire; some fires just need to burn themselves out.

Francis: When I am faced with dealing with a conflict situation, avoidance usually seems to be the easiest way out for me. But I have found that that places the burden of having to do something about it in the future. The longer I put it off, the more difficult it is for me to have the courage to deal with it.

Ray: In most of the situations I have faced, avoidance has come back to haunt me. This happens most often when I avoid my own feelings related to conflict.

Rose: It's difficult for me to see how avoidance can be productive. As one who readily engages in conflict, I've been pondering Jesus' avoiding some conflict in order to retreat to the mountainside to pray. I can't tell you how many times I have "crashed" after a difficult conflict because I have expended so much energy.

Katie: Avoidance is my default approach to conflict. It's such a long-standing practice with me it often isn't a conscious choice. I have difficulty recognizing conflict; first I notice my lowered energy, then difficulty focusing on tasks or the inability to think productively. I experience a vague dread. This habit of avoidance produces inertia and procrastination.

Marie: My dominant style in dealing with conflict is avoidance. I know that hasn't always been a healthy choice. I have doubted my abilities to handle conflict and so I've avoided it. But I've begun to develop my skills to remain engaged in conflict resolution. I am learning to choose the style and role I play rather than falling back into old patterns.

Katie: When I'm avoiding confronting an issue, I use cleaning out the refrigerator as a coping mechanism. In my attempt to create order in the midst of some kind of chaos in my life, I often find renewed energy to deal with the real issue.

Hannah: I've been thinking about how we all perceive things so differently. It is important to really attend to people, and to think carefully about what we say when we're tired. That may be a time to avoid a conflicted encounter.

Ray: Avoidance can be a very delicate line to tread and may not always end up as we plan. If we do plan to avoid a conflict we must first understand and measure all possible outcomes of doing or not doing so.

Alan: I'm wondering if conflict really *can* be avoided. Even if I choose to not get involved in a conflict because it doesn't involve me, by making this choice I am engaged at some level. I also recognize that avoidance behavior can be wrong. It's important to name that. Perhaps it is because of insecurity, indifference, or because we feel inadequate and don't want to "open a can of worms." Whether our choice to avoid conflict is negative or positive, we have made a choice.

Beth: Avoidance is complicated. When is there ever enough information to make an educated choice? So much injustice continues while good-hearted people sit back and just "learn" about it. However, action without reflection can seriously set back any positive change.

Annika: I find myself asking two questions that measure whether I should avoid acting for now or not: "Why am I doing this?" and "What will it do to those around me?"

Beth: This brings up the importance of clear vision and purpose. Will this action or inaction be effective or helpful? Is this issue the one that needs to be addressed right now or never? What is God's will in this? What are my agendas in this situation?

Hannah: Sometimes I avoid dealing with a conflict in a relationship and by so doing continue to hold a grudge. When we hold on to the actions of another, and in our silence cannot forgive, we are saying that their sins against us are larger and more powerful than what Jesus did on the cross. We are saying that Jesus died but these sins are not included in that saving act.

Rose: Jesus did not avoid the cross. He takes his followers to a new understanding of God's mission of ridding the world of violence. I am empowered to consider the need for avoidance in order to get out of the way for healing to occur and to get out of the way for people to nurture others in the midst of conflict. This is a strong message for me to sit with for quite awhile!

Building a Cohesiveness for Collaboration

Avoidance of difficult subjects can stand in the way of growth in the congregation, and people may keep conversation at a superficial or mundane level as a mask. However, we need to be careful not to label all talk "about the weather" as superficial. For one thing, the weather may be an important topic on a particular day and a farmer's livelihood may be made or broken because of it. Communities need social bonding and small talk helps provide this. A congregation that is always dealing with conflict will wear its members out. Only an exceptional few people thrive on conflict. Avoiding contentious conversation through common courtesy provides basic human connection that holds communities together. [8] Such cohesiveness can provide a fabric strong enough to engage conflict in a collaborative way.

How Avoidance Can Be Used in Helpful Ways

To avoid buys time, provides a cooling-off period, and gives distance when a conflict is spreading. Avoidance, like the other responses to conflict we will cover later in the book, cannot be used alone. To stop a spreading conflict, the leader may need to take control and be directive. He or she does that in order to provide opportunity for everyone to avoid direct confrontation for a specific period of time.

We are advised to avoid conflict if the issue is of low priority. The difficulty with that advice is that what may be low priority to one person may be of ultimate concern to another. [9] A ministerial leader can help a group avoid full engagement with an issue until there is more equal motivation on the part of all. In the meantime, that leader may need to carefully listen to the values of the different individuals and groups, providing encouragement for those who are anxious to deal with the issue now, and information for those who do not yet understand the importance of the issue to others.

Avoidance can be used when a congregation has established a

pattern of fighting that they repeat over and over again no matter what the issue. The church council might collaboratively decide to purposely *not* address a new conflict in order to disrupt the pattern. To leave an issue alone can help a congregation set a new pattern of seeing that some issues indeed *do* just go away by themselves. [10] Then, also collaboratively, the group will need to set a new pattern lest the old one simply reappears.

Avoidance of External Conflict

Each year thousands of people leave their congregations, either slipping quietly away or directly requesting their names be taken off the membership roles. When asked the reason, "Too much conflict!" is an all too frequent answer. These people may not be the primary parties in a conflict but merely bystanders. As bystanders they may more clearly see how harmful the contention is becoming. One could say these people are avoiding conflict. Should they? Is the alternative a broadening conflict in which they, too, become embroiled? Is there another alternative?

Through talking about avoidance we may discover that people begin to use it less as a default behavior. Then we can identify negative and positive uses of avoidance and gain skill in communicating effectively. By collaboratively discerning appropriate timing for avoidance and engagement of conflict we may help the entire congregation claim their appropriate role in being able to become more comfortable with a variety of responses to conflict, which we shall explore in the next chapters. [11]

Personal Reflection
How have you used avoidance as a default position? Why? What new insights do you have about how you might use avoidance as a purposeful response?

Collegial Conversation
Discuss a situation in your faith community that might be dealt with better by using avoidance appropriately now. How will you

do that? What role should each of you play? What effect might this have in the community?

Notes

1. Some authors of books on conflict insist that avoidance is always a bad response. Some authors include avoidance but consider it less useful than confrontation. Speed B. Leas in *Discover Your Conflict Management Style* (Washington, D.C.: Alban, 1997), pp. 18-20, includes "avoid," "ignore," "accommodate," and "flee" together in one strategy adding, "The most serious problem with this cluster of conflict strategies is that they don't change anything—and usually they don't help" (p. 20).

2. Joyce L. Hocker and William W. Wilmot, *Interpersonal Conflict*, 6th ed. (Boston: McGraw-Hill, 2001), pp. 135-45. The authors discuss the "twin cycles of avoidance," both of which begin with issues not being addressed—one that involves more avoidance and one that involves escalation of attack. Both lead to issues not being resolved and then to the cycle beginning all over again (pp. 137-38).

3. While many books on conflict management give little weight to "avoidance," a number of books on spirituality do. See Joyce Sequichie Hifler, *A Cherokee Feast of Days* (Tulsa, Okla.: Council Oaks Books, 1992). "Why be the other half of disagreement? Even an animal is smart enough not to run into . . . a trap. Most arguments are traps of one kind or another. . . . Let go, and realize that what is happening should be avoided like poison. The argument or disagreement is on the other side—leave it there" (p. 120).

4. These are but a few examples, and mostly from Luke.

5. Marshall Shelley, ed., *Leading Your Church Through Conflict and Reconciliation* (Minneapolis: Bethany, 1997), p. 179.

6. Dave Peters, *Surviving Church Conflict* (Scottdale, Pa.: Herald Press, 1997), pp. 73-74. Peters gives an example of needing to point out when someone is deliberately "sidetracking" a conflict by trying to change the subject.

7. Shelley, *Leading Your Church Through Conflict and Reconciliation*, pp. 210-22. This author uses only the image of "war" for conflict in chapter 21, and therefore sees determining if the war is "winnable" as the only use of avoidance.

8. Katie Day, *Difficult Conversations: Taking Risks, Acting with Integrity* (Bethesda, Md.: Alban, 1997), pp. 21-27.

9. Keith Huttenlocker, *Conflict and Caring: Preventing, Managing and Resolving Conflict in the Church* (Newburgh, Ind.: Trinity Press, 1988), pp. 28-31.

10. Ibid. "Problems frequently arise in the church which, although unpleasant for the time being, will soon pass. It is better to ignore them than create a long-term problem as a result of an unnecessary confrontation" (p. 29). There are always some risks to this strategy.

11. Speed Leas, *Discover Your Conflict Management Style* (Washington, D.C.: Alban, 1997). Leas combines "avoiding" with "accommodating" and adds five other styles: persuading, compelling, collaborating, negotiating, and supporting.

CHAPTER SEVEN

CONFRONTATION

To confront is to stand against, to stand face-to-face. Confronting may mean facing an issue that has been avoided. It may mean bringing forth an issue that for the sake of justice needs to be addressed boldly and publicly. Confrontation need not be a standoff; it can be an opportunity to see eye-to-eye. Having looked straight at one another, with our vast differences, we may be able to see more clearly. [1] Standing together, collaboratively, we may be able to face our mission and ministry with new vision.

One should use confrontation not simply because one has the power and ability to do so, or to reinforce one's self-image of identity or office. The goal of confrontation is to foster direct dialogue, to engage in a reciprocal search for truth, and to talk honestly about issues as part of a mutually accountable relationship. [2]

In order for confrontation to be real and honest and life-giving, we need to consider our own particular images and experiences of confrontation. We need to address issues of power. In this chapter we shall explore some biblical examples of confrontation. We will look at confrontational approaches with the goal of increasing our skill in using confrontation appropriately and carefully.

Images and Experiences of Confrontation

Should we ever cause conflict on purpose? The closest we get to a yes is in this chapter. Confrontation may be viewed as courageous or it may be viewed as imperialistic. How do you image confrontation? What emotions does it bring up in you?

To confront may be imaged as to "bring to the surface." We reveal that which was hidden. For some people confrontation is the very opposite of—perhaps the antidote to—avoidance. People will often deny painful issues as long as possible. Whereas leaders or principal parties may recognize a conflict months before it comes to the surface, bystanders may not. "I was shocked," they say when finally they are confronted with the reality of the conflict. The inability to confront conflict impedes dealing with the issue. The issue may be buried unresolved; underground it may not be dead at all, simply spreading its roots only to spring up some other place.[3]

Parishioners may refuse to see unless and until they themselves are hurt or betrayed. Congregation members may turn on the leaders who surface a conflict, even if they are not the ones who have caused the problem. As ministerial leaders we will frequently need to "bring something up" so that the congregation can become appropriately involved and work toward a collaborative solution.

Kevin, a pastor of a midsize congregation, responds to the very word *confrontation* negatively. For him it conjures up images of disappointment, judgment, unresolved anxiety, and broken or damaged relationships. He says, "Confrontation can be like a ketchup stain on a white shirt that becomes embedded in the fibers, altering its appearance regardless of efforts to wash it away." For him confrontation requires a significant amount of emotional energy that leaves emotional residue. Yet he realizes that confrontation is part of life, certainly in ministry, and that avoiding confrontation is unrealistic. Understanding this, Kevin is beginning to see confrontation in a new light: "My perception of confrontation will be re-created into a means of responding in a healthy way to conflict."

Ron is a diaconal minister in a congregation in the midst of transition. Confrontation requires courage to speak and fortitude to hear the response. Ron believes that being clear and centered in oneself and in what one believes protects one from too much pain in hearing out another person. This gives dignity for others to express themselves without interference from one's own anxiety or anger. Ron says, "The challenge for me is not to become enmeshed in a conflict without first confronting myself."

Sandra is an experienced pastor. "'Out-spoken,' 'honest,' 'confrontational,' 'opinionated'—these are labels people put on me at various points in my adolescence and young adulthood. At times I felt quite honored to be seen as someone honest enough to confront. At other times I felt cursed." Sandra kept growing through the years and became wiser with each situation of conflict. She discovered that her words have weight. She says she has learned to confront with her ears as well as her mouth, and that her gift of honesty can be used to serve. She now asks herself, "Through my words of confrontation and listening, am I offering life-giving service that builds and heals and leaves others free to claim their own power? Do I see Christ in the mirror after a time of confrontation or do I see only myself? Have I grown in knowing when and when not to confront?"

Gary, a gentle, strong pastor says, "Deciding to truly stand face-to-face with another, to be truly present for the other and for one's self, may be a very intimate moment." Can it be that confrontation is actually a form of intimacy? He asks, "Do we avoid confrontation because we may be afraid of getting too close to another? Too close to our own conflicted feelings?" Gary believes that true confrontation opens us up to being changed ourselves. One must really listen to the other's understanding of the conflict. He suggests beginning with, "I'm feeling there is some tension between us because of this issue. Since I value our relationship, this concerns me. Would you be willing to tell me your understanding of the issue? Would you also be willing to hear my understanding? Then perhaps we can work together on this. Why don't you begin? Let's take as much time as we need to truly hear each other."

For Reflection

1. Recall one or more situations in which a conflict was finally confronted. What was your role? What were your fears? In retrospect, what was gained? What was damaged?

2. Are you hesitant to open up a subject for fear that people (including yourself) will be hurt? Are you wary that you may open up wounds you do not have the skill to heal? Once you see an issue that needs to be engaged, do you want to confront the issue right away, therefore getting ahead of the process and the people? Be honest: what are your skills and your difficulties with confrontation?

The Issue of Power

If to confront is to stand against, face-to-face, we must examine power differentials. [4] A powerful person, group, or nation can easily choose direct confrontation because they have the power to prevail. With such power they may not even realize how others experience this confrontation. The pastor may or may not have substantial power within the congregation, yet knowing who has is an invaluable tool when using confrontation. Smaller nations, a staff person with less status, a congregational member with less formal education or expertise may be reluctant to use confrontation, at least *direct* confrontation.

There are many kinds of power: [5]

- Power of physical size
- Power of office
- Power of experience
- Power of money
- Power of gender, race, class
- Power of education
- Power of voice
- Power of expertise
- Power of resources
- Power of . . .

What power do you have? How do you exercise it? What power intimidates you? Which kinds of power do you use to confront? Which kinds of power are you reluctant to use?

Some people who claim confrontation as their primary means of responding to conflict do so easily because they clearly have power, for example, of office or economic resources. They simply confront when things are not to their liking and they unilaterally determine the outcome of that confrontation. They may be congratulated for being able to handle any conflict decisively, but different voices that might contribute to creative solving of the conflict are never heard. They may stand shoulder-to-shoulder with a person, but they never really see the other's face; they never see eye-to-eye.

However, if one thinks of confrontation as facing an issue *together*, with genuine collaboration, people need to use shared power. Power in this case belongs to the collaborative relationship rather than just to one individual. This power is integrative power, which creatively comes up with a solution that might be totally new. [6] We will come back to the subject of power in chapters 8 and 9 when we consider the responses to conflict of "compete" and "control."

Biblical Images of Confrontation

Here are a few biblical examples of confrontation:

Genesis 4:8-10: God said to Cain, "Where is your brother Abel?" Abel responds to the confrontational question, "Am I my brother's keeper?" to which God asks, "What have you done?"

2 Samuel 12:1-15: God sent Nathan to David to confront him. Nathan uses a story and in verse 7 he says to David, "You are the man!"

John 2:13-22: We hear the vivid account of Jesus' making a whip, overturning the tables, and driving out the moneychangers. (See also Matt. 21:12-13; Mark 11:15-17; Luke 19:45.) Read on and see that Jesus' confrontation was met with the chief priests and scribes seeking a way to destroy Jesus—for they *feared* him.

Jesus was often confronted with a question:

Mark 7:5: "Why do your disciples not live according to the tradition of the elders, but eat with defiled hands?"

Mark 9:16: Jesus to the disciples and the crowd: "What are you arguing about with them?"

Mark 10:18: Jesus to the man who was rich who was trying to justify himself: "Why do you call me good?"

Jesus' entire life and ministry was a confrontation with mere religiosity, with demons, with those who would stand in the way of the reign of God. He was a gentle, kind healer, *and* he was direct and purposeful. He realized that the way to the cross involved conflict and that his death was the final conflict. He did not confront the disciples, his religious opponents, or even death itself for the sheer pleasure or glory of it. His reluctance is epitomized in Mark 14:36: "Abba . . . remove this cup from me; yet, not what I want, but what you want." For Christ, confrontation was a means of seeking and following the will of God.

Productive Confrontation

Whereas to avoid may be to delay, to confront is to begin. It may be the first stage of conflict, or, more accurately, the first stage of mutual recognition and active engagement with conflict. How one confronts—how one begins—is very important.

> *True confrontation opens us up to being changed ourselves.*

Will confrontation lead to healthy engagement and eventual productive outcomes? Will confrontation intimidate, driving one party away or the conflict itself underground? Will confrontation overpower in such a way that, although drawing the conflict seemingly to a quick conclusion, the end result leaves one party defeated and one the conqueror? Will confrontation ultimately strengthen collaborative relationships?

When considering confrontation, we must realize that sometimes we *are confronted* and sometimes we choose *to confront*. In either case, we cannot control the reactions of other people; we need to be responsible for our own actions. We can be prayerfully thoughtful in trying to engage in confrontation in healthy ways.

Jonathan's confrontation of David in the Bible led to repentance: "I have sinned against the LORD" (2 Sam. 12:13). For centuries churches have included David's Psalm 51 in worship services. His words become our own as we stand before God and one another with our need for confrontation, conviction, and conversion.

Unhelpful Confrontation (And What You Can Do About It)

We all have experienced someone confronting us, sometimes in healthy productive ways, sometimes not. You may recognize yourselves and others in the examples below:

"Are you trying to start something?" (picking a fight).

"I find you to be arrogant" (character judgment).

"This situation has gotten clearly out of hand. The leadership is totally inadequate" (ascribing blame).

"Are you sitting down?" (intended to prepare people, but often raising anxiety).

"While we're at it, maybe we should talk about who took the flag out of the sanctuary" (intended either to take the spotlight off one's own offenses or to escalate the conflict).

"Whose church is this, mine or yours?" (intended to polarize).[7]

If confrontation begins in a less-than-helpful way, one can respond:

- By ignoring, thereby choosing avoidance (which could be either a good or bad choice).
- By taking a deep breath and gathering your own thoughts first.
- By retaliating in kind (thereby escalating the conflict— helpful if the conflict should be escalated, but not helpful when it leads to mutual character assassination).

- By facing the confrontation but deliberately changing the focus. (This could be by a question, or an affirmation of the issue, or some other appropriate response. This change will need to be accepted or it will be viewed as avoidance.)
- By directly addressing the confrontation but separating issues from persons. (This can be productive but is less helpful when the type of conflict is intrapersonal or interpersonal.)

Here are some helpful responses to the examples above:

"Are you trying to start something?" "Yes, I am. I believe we should start addressing the causes of the problems between us."

"I find you to be arrogant." "I'm sorry you have experienced me that way. I would like to sit down with you and discuss the issues between us."

"The situation has gotten clearly out of hand. The leadership is totally inadequate." "I agree that the atmosphere is pretty tense in the congregation right now" (acknowledging the concern but reframing the assessment). "What are some of the things you have been noticing about the community right now?" (bypassing the oblique criticism of particular people but exercising leadership in the confrontation).

"Are you sitting down?" Either sit down or remain standing and say, "I need to know right now!"

"While we're at it, maybe we should talk about who took the flag out of the sanctuary." "That *is* a controversial subject. For the moment, let's return to the problem at hand."

"Whose church is this, mine or yours?" "It's God's church and all of us are differently gifted members of the Body of Christ."

Problems That May Arise

What if you are blindsided, hit unprepared for confrontation? What if you are taken by surprise? What if you are so hurt by what is said that you lose your objectivity and your emotions begin to run wild?

If the conflict is interpersonal, confrontation in front of a larger group is unfair. It undermines a person's authority to minister effectively in the larger community. When that happens to a leader, she or he needs to acknowledge what was said, but not abdicate power to the confronting person. By calmly stating that this conversation needs to take place at another time and place (and then following up to do so), the leader retains his or her role and identity. Handling this situation gracefully may even enhance the respect the group has for the leader.

Confrontation needs to be done orally in person, if at all possible. Many have come to regret their own words put on paper, which are subject to misinterpretation and might be used later out of context. E-mail, with its quick response time, is even more tempting. Sending any confrontational e-mail while one is angry will probably cause more problems than it solves.

Since the probable response to critical confrontation is defensiveness, although dialogue is the goal, the person confronted may not be able to engage in objective conversation right then. [8] To move beyond a self-protective posture, he or she will need affirmation as well as honesty, and space to regain composure—particularly if the confrontation was a surprise.

We may be approaching a situation with courage to confront, but functioning with inadequate information or false assumptions. On one hand, we need to ask and to consult appropriately in order for confrontation to be wise and useful. On the other hand, confronting a person who has faulty or incomplete information may prevent problematic delays or embarrassment later.

Helpful Confrontation Strategies

How, then, can we begin—confront—in ways that lead to healthy engagement of the issues and of one another? Even though we have carefully planned what we believe to be a healthy confrontational statement, we must recognize that it may not be received the way we intended. For example:

"I have noticed what seems to be a change in the nature of our relationship. Is there some problem here that I am missing?" (low-key engagement). "I want you to know that I care about our relationship."

"I have been hearing that there is misunderstanding (distrust, conflict, and so forth) between the groups that use the fellowship hall on Thursday evenings" (observation). "I would like to invite the two groups or leaders of the two groups to sit down and talk about it" (invitation and offer to serve in the role of mediator).

"I have heard there is some misunderstanding about the proposed changes. Would it be possible to move this issue to the front of our meeting so that we can have open conversation now?" (promoting early confrontation so that contention does not seep out through other topics on the agenda).

"The charges and countercharges that have been going on must stop" (direct intervention as a way to begin a different level of conversation).

"I observe that we have been talking around the core issue for almost an hour. I think we should address the real reason we are here" (guidance from avoidance to facing the issue).

"May I tell you something about myself? When I hear you casually use the Lord's name in vain (make condescending comments about an individual or race of people, and so forth) I become very uncomfortable" (noting the problem, opening the door for deeper issues, but beginning with one's own perspective).

Confront when:

- The time is right, not just in the heat of the moment.
- You are ready with information.
- You can face an issue or look a person in the eye and hear the truth.
- Power differentials do not hinder a just outcome. [9]
- You can meet in a neutral, safe place.
- The situation requires immediate attention to prevent escalation or danger.

Ways to confront: [10]

- When possible, confront in the first person.
- Do not confront on behalf of others.
- Be direct and gentle.
- Keep confrontation in the present.
- Confront the behavior, not the person.
- Do not interpret behavior.

When choosing confrontation remember:

- To consider how the person you are confronting may perceive your position of authority.
- To anticipate a various range of reactions to the confrontation.
- To understand frustration, which builds from a series of irritations.
- To try not to undermine other people's integrity or make them feel small or outnumbered.
- To carefully select words, tone of voice, location, and time of confrontation.
- That action without reflection causes more harm than good, and that reflection without action is futile.

The Courage to Confront

Confrontation takes courage. After long prayerful careful consideration the moment may present itself.

Birmingham bus no. 2857 is now restored in the Henry Ford Village in Dearborn, Michigan. That was the bus in which Rosa Parks sat down, thereby standing up to centuries of discrimination. Some say she was tired and therefore refused to move when directed by the driver to relinquish her seat to a white man. But she had been part of what would become the Civil Rights movement before that. Her action that day was both spontaneous and strategic. Sometimes we know precisely when confrontation will start something; sometimes it may be part of a series of almost everyday acts.

The Role of the Church

After any disaster in the community, nation, or the world, news reporters turn their microphones toward religious leaders. "What are you doing to comfort the victims and their families?" The role of the church is perceived to be to console not to confront.

And yet confront we must. Local congregations must confront issues of hunger, poverty, homelessness, and more in order to address societal problems. The prophetic role of the church demands active engagement in conflicted situations. Grassroots networks of faithful people take on issues that no one individual or congregation can address alone. Church bodies have taken public stands on injustices in society. What are some examples of prophetic confrontation you have experienced in the church? When have you exercised leadership in confrontation? What were the risks? What were the dangers? What were the outcomes?

The role of the church is not always clear. Churches themselves are frequently in conflict with one another over societal issues. To confront an issue may bring a faith community into direct opposition with other congregations in the community, or with the judicatory or church body. Such direct engagement is very likely to stir up conflict at many levels within the congregation. Church leaders need prayerful discernment as they set forth to confront public issues and guide their communities faithfully through turmoil.

The history of the church reveals brave, strong confrontational stands. It also reveals misguided crusades that caused untold suffering. Misuse of ecclesial power contributes to colonization in the name of mission. There has often been a narrow line between evangelization, which intends to give life, and "conquering for Christ," which enslaves or annihilates. One needs to seriously ask, what is the conflict? What or whom is one confronting? Is one confronting sources of oppression and not just personal adversaries? What are the means of confrontation? How has the death and resurrection of Christ changed the very nature of confrontation?

Personal Reflection

Take time to recall your own journey of faith in the midst of conflict. How has confrontation served you and the people you serve well? What wounds of past confrontation still need healing? What skillful use of confrontation do you want to continue to develop?

Collegial Conversation

Talk about some confrontation phrases that have been said to you. Brainstorm appropriate and productive responses. Try out some phrases you each might use to confront a new situation that needs to be addressed. Discuss how those might be heard. Continue to explore together how you as colleagues or how your congregation might engage in mutually accountable confrontation.

Notes

1. Loughlan Sofield and Carroll Juliano, *Collaboration: Uniting Our Gifts in Ministry* (Notre Dame, Ind.: Ave Maria Press, 2000), pp. 139-46.

2. Ibid., pp. 140-41.

3. Dave Peters, *Surviving Church Conflict* (Scottdale, Pa.: Herald Press, 1997), pp. 72-73.

4. Joyce L. Hocker and William W. Wilmot, *Interpersonal Conflict,* 6th ed. (Boston: McGraw-Hill, 2001), pp. 95-128. The authors note differing orientations to power and help the reader assess power in a relational view.

5. Ibid., p. 76. Hocker and Wilmot list "power currencies": resource control, interpersonal linkages, and expertise (p. 108).

6. Ibid., p. 96.

7. Joseph Phelps, *More Light, Less Heat* (San Francisco: Jossey-Bass, 1999), pp. 28-33. Phelps emphasizes that dialogue is not debate.

8. Sofield and Juliano, *Collaboration*, p. 141.

9. Hugh F. Halverstadt, *Managing Church Conflict* (Louisville: Westminster John Knox, 1991), pp. 122-30. Halverstadt describes changing contextual factors in surfacing a new conflict to balance power ratios.

10. Sofield and Juliano, *Collaboration*, pp. 142-43. This list is taken directly from Sofield and Juliano. Their chapter "Confrontation" is very helpful (pp. 139-46).

CHAPTER EIGHT

COMPETITION

I f, for some, confrontation energizes, then competition really gets the juices going. Competition is but one style of engaging conflict. For many in our society it may be the habitual response. For others competition seems the very antithesis of collaboration, especially in the church. Is competition a good thing? Are we made disciples of Christ in order to compete with the world? Are we called to conquer for Christ? Is competition inevitable? The church in the United States, which may be suspicious of competition as a way of dealing with conflict, dwells in a society that highly regards competition. This compels us to take a very close look at the competitive response to conflict.

Personal History with Competition

How competitive are you? Some of us may be more competitive than we think. Some people who have competed successfully in athletics, the arts, or academics may take that into church as a way to settle differences of opinion. And some who compete energetically in contests may separate that completely from strategies of addressing conflict in their lives. What is your own personal history with competition? In a conflict, are you quick to compete to win? Has your experience of losing been so formative that you assume you have little power or skill in using competition? Among the various responses to conflict our own personal histories with *competition* play a very strong role. It is worth taking the time to reflect on our experiences with competition at various stages of our lives. [1]

Faith Perspectives

Not only is it helpful to look at our own history with competition, but we also gain insight from thinking about the basic beliefs of the Christian faith. However, even within Christianity we find differing perspectives in regard to competition.

The God Who Creates

How did God create us to be? (Genesis 1–2). Is competition part of creation or of the Fall? Is it "natural"? Were we created to compete? Some would cite "survival of the fittest." Some would say not only were we created to compete, but that it is necessary for human life. Others respond that competition leads to harm, even death. Some say that competition to the death is beneficial, even necessary, in a world of scarce resources. Others point out that numerous United Nations and other studies show that when there is enough food for survival and when people have life choices, birth rates go down and all can survive. [2]

God created the world and human beings in it for life-giving interdependence. Competition can be a means to help individuals and communities develop their full potential. However, when we trust in the Creator Provider God we do not need to use competition as a way of life to have our needs met. That trust allows us to put limits on the means and degree to which we compete. [3] We do not need to be number one.

The God Who Serves and Reconciles

Did Christ engage in competition? If so, with whom or why? God incarnate redefined competition. He came not to overwhelm, or to overpower, or to use his strength and position to win arguments and battles for himself. Jesus turned competition upside down. He said that whoever wants to be great must be servant of all. Can you imagine what kind of world this would be if people competed to see who could serve the most? (Mark 10:43). He welcomed children and said the reign of God belongs to them, the lowest members of society. He ate with tax collectors and sinners. He was victorious, but not over human beings—not even his enemies. He conquered death, but not for his own sake. When he arose on Easter Sunday he did not say, "I won! I'm home free; forget about the losers." Matthew 28:7 reads, "Go quickly and tell his disciples, 'He has been raised from the dead, and indeed he is going ahead of you to Galilee; there you will see him.' " The core of resurrection life in not competition, but community.

There are those who claim that Jesus was a terrific competitor, fishing for souls and with the religious leaders. To this, author Bill Diehl says, "Rubbish." When the disciples sought to settle conflict through competing for Jesus' favor, Jesus said that whoever would be first must be a slave (Matt. 20). Diehl writes, "Jesus lived and moved in a competitive society just as we do. But he was not hooked by the powers of competition. He did not *need* to compete." [4]

The God Who Empowers the Church Through the Spirit

The Acts and Epistles are full of accounts of the young church in conflict. In contrast, consider the Body of Christ imagery: "God has so arranged the body, giving the greater honor to the inferior member, that there may be no dissension within the body, but the members may have the same care for one another. If one member suffers, all suffer together with it; if one member is honored, all rejoice together with it" (1 Cor. 12:24b-26). Paul wrote, "If we live by the Spirit, let us also be guided by the Spirit"; and advising against competition, "Let us not become conceited, competing against one another, envying one another" (Gal. 5:25-26).

The "armor of God" passage (Eph. 6:10-20) could lead one to

embrace competition. However, Paul urges people not to compete to the death, but to be "strong in the Lord," to persevere, keep alert, and be bold as ambassadors of the gospel. He also turns competition around: "Love one another with mutual affection; outdo one another in showing honor" (Rom. 12:10).

Competition as a Way of Life

The American Way

But competition is the "American way," people argue. Our financial and political systems are built on competition. We have an adversarial legal system. It is the prosecuting attorney's job to make the case, to win for the state. It is the defense attorney's job to win for the defense. In this adversarial legal debate the real goal is to win, not necessarily to jointly search for the truth. The premise is that if each side is working as hard as they can the truth will emerge as determined by judge or jury, but that does not always happen.

Competitive sports, both amateur and professional, are a major part of American culture. Some believe this competitive spirit has always been part of American life; others feel it is increasing at alarming rates. To some, winning isn't only part of the game, it is the only thing that matters. Watching a good match is entertainment, but how does being competitive shape the way we live in community with our differences? When does competition go too far?

On the job, some managers encourage "healthy conflict" among individual workers, saying this will encourage production and sales. A free-enterprise system is based on competition. And if in the battle over customers one salesperson or company fades from the scene, so much the better. In the church, even though our mission goals may never be stated the way they are in corporate America, in the midst of conflict churches often compete with one another—even to the death of a congregation or a church body.

The Argument Culture

Deborah Tannen in her book *The Argument Culture* writes that in this culture "nearly everything is framed as a battle or game in which winning or losing is the main concern. These all have their uses and their place, but they are not the only way—and often not the best way—to understand and approach our world." [5]

When we decide to seek truth by setting up a battle between two sides, we believe that every issue has two sides—no more, no less. But competition does not lead to truth when an issue is not composed of two opposing sides but is a complex mixture of many views. Often the truth is in the midst, not in the oversimplified extremes.

"The argument culture limits the information we get rather than broadening it in another way. When a certain kind of interaction is the norm, those who feel comfortable with that type of interaction are drawn to participate, and those who do not feel comfortable with it recoil and go elsewhere. . . . When a problem is posed in a way that polarizes, the solution is often obscured before the search is under way." [6]

Competition in the Church

Because the American culture is so highly attuned to competition, and because members of congregations live in and are influenced by the culture, very quickly members on competing sides of a conflict may become more interested in who won than the actual mission of the church, which both sides are pursuing. [7] Who won or lost in a church conflict may be remembered for years to come.

Religion in America has not escaped the compete-to-win syndrome. Too often the "best" clergy are those who can "pack 'em in" on Sunday morning. [8] Churches compete for members. Churches and individual Christian leaders compete to win doctrinal debates. Can there be healthy competition among and within churches? In what ways is competition a detriment to living in Christian community? "A competitive, or 'power over,' style is characterized by aggressive and uncooperative behavior—pursuing your own concerns at the expense of another."[9]

The paragraphs above may lead one to believe that competition is always unhealthy and therefore of no use to the church. But, remember, we began with the statement that competition energizes. It can clarify issues. It can tone muscles. It can help people develop their skills. However, the death of dialogue may not be the optimum solution to a conflict, especially if the powerlessness of the community is merely an illusion. A congregation in the midst of a conflict may fear it is too fragile to engage in healthy debate, but if a safe environment is set so that the issues can be discussed with insight and clarity, that congregation may well discover it is not only energized, but empowered to move ahead in mission.

How might competition provide a positive way to deal with conflict? "A competitive style of managing conflict is productive if one competes to accomplish individual goals without destroying the other person."[10] Competition can inform the other of one's degree of commitment to an issue. We can look at competition as a valued, even the best, response in *some* situations.

Competition as a Response to Conflict

Compete when:

- The issue is important enough that the church cannot afford to lose.
- The issue is unimportant enough that to win or lose is insignificant.
- A decision cannot be delayed; an action must be taken, such as in an emergency.
- Compromise is not yet possible.
- Relationships and trust are well established.
- An authoritative presence can ensure a fair and open competition.
- All participants believe a safe environment has been established.

- People can agree to debate an issue, not a person's worth.
- Competition potentially can lead to creative solutions.

Refuse to compete when:

- There are more than two outcomes, not just pro and con.
- Competition causes people to lose their sense of value and decency.
- Power is not balanced.
- Only some of the parties enjoy competition.
- Some people are unfairly advantaged.
- There is no leader or place to ensure a "fair" fight.
- Competition will escalate the conflict rather than clarify issues.
- Other strategies to address the conflict could be more productive.
- Winning and losing in the moment will be remembered for years to come.

Setting a Safe Environment for Competition

Setting and maintaining a trustworthy environment where people feel physically and emotionally safe is important in a conflicted situation. It is particularly needed when competition is the chosen method of response. A primary role a leader can play is to use his or her authority to ensure an environment of calm, respect, and openness to opposing points of view. If the conflict is *about* the leader, if staff is competing with one another, or if the leader has strong opinions and is engaged in competition to win, it will be difficult, if not impossible, for the leader to also play the role of referee or even to use his or her authority effectively in keeping the environment neutral. Others, such as a regional church leader, may need to provide this role. But for the most part it will be the pastor's role to exercise kind and wise authoritative leadership to insist that people are respectful and fair so that people truly feel the atmosphere is safe and trustworthy.

Collaborative Competition

Among the ways to deal with conflict, competition can be particularly contentious. But even competition can be collaborative when all parties willingly choose to engage in it. To collaboratively choose includes selecting competition from other alternatives as the best means. To collaborate in competition necessitates exploring and dealing with power differentials. To collaboratively compete means the group will work to maintain a safe environment, to set and adhere to guidelines for engagement, and to agree upon what losing and winning the competition will mean for the community. This can be done. Pastors and other leaders should continuously be working to establish and maintain such a healthy environment for all collaborative work and learning. Then dialogue and healthy debate will be natural and productive.

Developing Skills to Compete

Make no mistake; I am not trying to dissuade people from using competition. It may be the most helpful and life-giving strategy for dealing with a given conflict in a specific situation. There are numerous books, many in the business and sports worlds, on the subject.[11] Interestingly, such books are not as provocative as their titles and opponents might suggest. They offer ways to survive—even thrive—amid fierce competition and constant change.

Competition can be addictive.

Competition, however, can be addictive. People often invest an enormous amount of mental, physical, and emotional energy to compete. We need to pay close attention to the formative role of competition in our personal histories, as well as in the communal history of the congregation. What skills has a congregation used to compete in the past? How healthy or destructive have they been? We need to ask, "Why am I—are we—doing this and what will it do to others?"

Sometimes the participants in dealing with conflict through competition are fine, but the rest of the room becomes frustrated or anxious, or actually clears out. Bystanders can also contribute to an unhealthy use of competition when they set parties into motion against one another for the entertainment of the audience.

The pastor needs to be skilled in using competition and in discerning when to use it and how. Sometimes the best way to deflate a dangerous competition is for participants to recognize the game's essential oppressive nature and to change their approach.

A congregation does not often *choose* competition to deal with conflict; however, people within congregations, including their leaders, often bring their competitive selves *to* the conflict. In order not to succumb to an automatically competitive response in the midst of conflict, whenever possible it is helpful when entering a conversation or meeting to be aware of what sides to an issue may be present. (This is not always possible because conflict doesn't occur by appointment only.) Then we can be already aware of arguments and secondary motives that may be informing those sides and can discern our own investment in the issues, both personal and professional. Rather than having to deal with unexamined conflict, we can then plan strategies for coping with the competition. That will avoid unhelpfully diffusing it, or allowing people to utilize it for their own personal advantage. In planning to use competition in a helpful way, there are a number of methods to consider.

Methods to Compete

Debate

When facing an issue of conflict, a good way to foster collaboration is to engage in a lively debate. Issues are clarified. Positions sharpened. I do not mean spontaneous debate without rules; random arguing often escalates the conflict and hurts people. A church council or adult or youth forum could arrange a specific time and neutral setting for parties to prepare for and engage in careful debate. Needed: A set time frame; well-balanced opposing sides; and a clear statement of the issue to be debated. One can then proceed with a set pattern. For example: a five-minute opening statement of positions from each side; two ten-minute rebuttal periods; and closing remarks. In this setting, deciding who won or lost the formal debate is less important than that competing ideas were clearly stated, fully explored, and ideas sharpened for the sake of healthy decision making.

Grading

Although this may seem strange to include in a book on church conflict, grading—used pervasively in the culture and frequently in the church—has an edge of conflict to it. Grading in a competitive culture often becomes competitive. Some Christian educators in the church use grading as a means of accountability and even as a means to motivate students to work hard. The pastor or Sunday school teacher may foster, intentionally or not, an atmosphere of being winners and losers. Students' gifts are set one against another rather than engaged collaboratively. Human beings are prone to measure themselves against one another, often negatively. Hence through the use of the competition inherent in grading, one may foster contentious conflict between people, and often conflict inside an individual. I find it difficult to make a case for grading in the Christian community. There are many more creative methods of teaching that one can use.

Contests

Purposely setting up a contest may help groups within a congregation strengthen their muscles. To have a "game night" or a sports Saturday where teams within the congregation engage in competition for the sake of enjoyment can help develop a collaborative spirit. What contests have you experienced that have built community? When might a contest to entertain (or raise money, and so forth) be unhealthy? Contests can be healthy when the issue is not important and winning is not the ultimate goal. There are all sorts of community-building contests that can make each person feel stronger and a more able member of the congregation. And they can be fun! One needs to be careful, however, that contests not be a facile means of motivation for new membership, because the result may be conflict where none was intended. The question should always be, *Is the method chosen congruent with the goal?*

Voting

Many congregations have a long-established pattern of deciding issues by vote. Congregational constitutions set the method of bringing items to an agenda—which conflicting issues need to be decided by a simple majority and which by two-thirds vote and so forth. Voting can become bitterly competitive and highly divisive. The winning side may have succeeded merely 51 percent to 49 percent; the losing side is left wondering what would have happened had their absent members' voices and votes been heard and counted. With good leadership that keeps the atmosphere healthy, voting can be clarifying and those on both sides of the vote can unify around the outcome.

A group may vote on issues over which there is no significant conflict. However, conflict may swirl around a congregation without ever coming to a vote. Using the vote as a way to resolve differences effectively requires a balance between short-term and long-term outcomes.

When a hot topic must be brought to a vote, discussion toward voting can be used effectively if speakers have time limits and the chair balances comments between those speaking in favor and those speaking against the issue. For example, at a regular congregational annual meeting, with the agenda publicly announced beforehand, a congregation faces the difficult issue of whether to sell some revered church property. If the leader carefully keeps the environment calm, gives equal opportunity for those for and those against selling to take turns making their case, once the vote is called for (and a vote will be necessary for this legal transaction), the group can make a difficult decision and feel good about the process.

One more example of a positive, communal way to compete: Although the privacy of the voting booth is a cherished right in a democracy every four years, the Iowa caucuses provide a public, communal way for people to express their preferences for their party's candidate for president. More than 120,000 citizens came together on a cold January night in 2004 at two thousand locations across the state. Some people knew one another; some were strangers. With a common structure under local leadership, people listened to one another's views, "voted" by moving to different corners of the room, and were counted. If one group was not viable (garnering 15 percent of the vote), people had to collaborate in their competition, working it out until the results could be telephoned to Des Moines and to the rest of the waiting country. Although the procedure was complicated and passions strong, in all of those two thousand locations there was not one incidence of violence, or even irresolvable confusion. Respect reigned. Public communal competition worked.

Sharing Experiences with Competition

Hannah: When I was young I was generally the last one picked for any type of game. I learned that competition was not fun. You had to be good to even play the game. As an adult, my husband encouraged me to run. I've learned to love it and for the first time have been told maybe I could have competed. However, I still cringe at the word *competition*. Even if it does not involve sports, I still fear I will lose and will feel like I felt when I was not picked for the team. I ponder what to do when someone in the church intentionally sets a conflict up for competition.

Beth: I view competition as potentially healthy and a helpful way to deal with some kinds of conflict, but I also hold competition in suspicion. On the one hand, although I am fully able to sit calmly and nicely dialogue about differences, I get more out of bantering. Competition increases awareness. But on the other hand, I put relationships ahead of winning. Sometimes I have backed down too quickly for the sake of a relationship. [12] Competition is like fire—essential and incredibly helpful, but dangerous.

Jessie: When I get into the thick of things, it is difficult to say to myself, "Wait a minute, Jessie, me thinkest thou dost compete." Forget that—I want to win!

Annika: I've learned how oppressive excessive competition can become. My friend and I played ourselves against each other. We turned our gifts into obsessions to gain control in opposition to those things we couldn't win. But lately we have begun to appreciate how divergent gifts work together in an almost symphonic orchestration. In that framework, competition is not only healthy, but drives the opus.

Bill: I believe it is helpful to compete when competition results in improved skills for all and for a better, collaborative, use of resources and gifts.

Rose: I'm a quiet competitor. I find my inner competition motivates me and drives me to achieve, accomplish, even excel. Competition moves me toward collaboration when I seek to work with others in accomplishing a task. But I feel called, especially in public ministry, to keep a check so that I remain balanced—strong, but driven by the Spirit to collaboratively deal with the conflict.

Ray: Sometimes competition is readily visible and in other cases it is present in ways we would not expect. I like to think of myself as not a competitor, but in reality I am. Competition can result in hurt feelings and even greater conflict. When the competition goes sour, the development of individuals and the community is put on hold, or even disintegrates.

Steve: I believe that setting a trustworthy environment is of utmost importance if we use competition as an approach to resolving conflict in the church. In a friendly competition, what makes it friendly is the environment in which it is played. That means ground rules.

Francis: Respect is crucial. In creating a safe environment to deal with conflict, we may need to create some physical distance.

Marie: I am trying to become more comfortable just dwelling in the midst of competition when it is positive, and letting it work. It can be helpful when all parties agree that the outcome will be good regardless of who "wins" or "loses." Even though I'm cautious about using competition as a strategy, I enjoy it when competition moves quickly to collaboration.

Personal Reflection

Explore your own history and feelings concerning competition. What skills do you have to compete? In what fields and arenas? How are you growing in ability to lead a group through conflict when competition is present? When, in your experience, is competition a freely chosen means of dealing with conflict?

Collegial Conversation

Discuss ways to set a trustworthy environment to use competition in healthy ways in your congregation. How might it invigorate people? How can you collaboratively work to maintain a safe environment for all voices to be heard and power balanced?

When there is conflict in your wider church body, how can you contribute to creative solutions?

Notes

1. Look once more at chapter 4, "Personal History of Conflict."
2. See Parker Palmer, *The Company of Strangers* (New York: Crossroad, 1981), for a discussion of competition over scarce resources.

3. See Edward de Bono, *I Am Right, You Are Wrong* (London: Viking, 1990). De Bono calls for creativity, originality, and an understanding of perception if we are to make a better future.

4. William E. Diehl, *Thank God It's Monday* (Philadelphia: Fortress Press, 1982), p. 40. Many Christians speak about the dangers of "unfair" competition, but few wrestle with the value of "competition" *per se*. Diehl does. See chapter 2, "Our Competitive Society"; chapter 3, "The Dark Side of Competition"; and chapter 4, "A Theology for a Competitive Society?" (pp. 17-51).

5. Deborah Tannen, *The Argument Culture* (New York: Random House, 1998), p. 4.

6. Ibid., pp. 20, 21.

7. Joseph Phelps, *More Light, Less Heat: How Dialogue Can Transform Christian Conflicts into Growth* (San Francisco: Jossey-Bass, 1999). "Debate denotes two clearly defined polarities about which each combatant argues in order to gain victory over the other. It is a win-lose battle" (p. 29).

8. Diehl, *Thank God It's Monday*, p. 29.

9. Joyce L. Hocker and William W. Wilmot, *Interpersonal Conflict*, 6th ed. (Boston: McGraw-Hill, 2001), p. 145.

10. Ibid.

11. For example, see Hal F. Rosenbluth and Diane McFerrin Peters, *Care to Compete? Secrets from America's Best Companies on Managing with People and Profits in Mind* (Reading, Mass.: Perseus Books, 1998).

12. More on "backing down" in chapter 10, "Accommodation."

CHAPTER NINE

CONTROL

H e's so controlling." Many of us abhor controlling people but fear things getting out of control. We have a dilemma. How am I to avoid being seen as a controlling person and yet exercise my authority in keeping conflict controlled so that it does not escalate? Likewise, the term *strong leader* has dual connotations. One might picture leaders sure of themselves, able to keep debate in conflicted situations orderly, "under control"; or as compulsive, overly managerial "control freaks."

This society and many churches in recent decades have moved from authoritarian leadership to shared power. Whereas that encourages the organization or faith community to exercise mutual accountability in dealing with differences, when conflict threatens to splinter a group people may express a wish for a return to what nostalgically may seem like the good old days when their leaders were "in control." Sometimes leaders want to do that themselves, seeing new styles as overly permissive. But reclaiming such control may undo years of progressive, collaborative team building.

However, having a pastor who exercises appropriate authority gives people confidence. This leader's very presence may signal not abuse, but security, and go a long way to defuse unhealthy conflict. Control can dominate, stifle creativity, and suffocate people and their ability to deal with conflict. Or control can bring order to chaos, security to craziness, and clarity to complexity.

Taking Charge

Think of an early time in your life when you were put in charge of something. Perhaps you were eight years old when your mother asked you to watch your two-year-old brother for a few minutes.

- Do you remember what happened?
- How did you feel? What did you do?
- How did it turn out? How did you feel then?

Remember a time when you first felt you could control things. Perhaps your parents or a Scout leader gave you the responsibility of making sure the van was packed with everyone's gear before a camping trip. There might have been a conflict over whose backpack went where; you were the one in charge and you took control of the situation.

- How did you handle the responsibility to deal with conflict?
- What thoughts and feelings went through your head?
- What skills did you use?

Remember a time when you felt out of control. In a voluntary or paid position during high school, college, or young adulthood you were in charge of leading people, but things didn't go as you had imagined. Things—people—got out of control.

- How did you feel?
- What did you do?
- What were you not able to do?

Remember conflict situations in which someone other than you was the leader.

- Have you ever felt controlled?
- Were there times when someone else was in control that you felt safe and empowered?
- Were there times when you felt cornered? Demeaned?
- How did the leader act? What did the leader do?
- Looking back, what might you have done?

Think of times today when you have the responsibility of leadership.

- Do you like being in charge? Why or why not?
- What leadership skills do you bring to situations of being in charge during a time of conflict?

Faith Perspectives About Control

God is omnipotent. We are not! Although we know that having absolute control over a situation or over people is idolatrous, sometimes we act otherwise. And yet God has given to human beings certain responsibilities as good stewards to care for the earth and its inhabitants. [1]

Saying, "God is in control," may or may not provide much comfort in times of serious conflict. People can perceive the world to be greatly out of control. God limits divine control in order to create a covenant relationship between God and God's people. But we can trust that God is still God and we cannot, nor need not, play God. However, leaving everything up to God or blaming God for human conflicts can allow us to sidestep our own responsibilities.

Throughout human history some people have assumed that God has given them a mandate to dominate. Therefore they try to justify taking total control of their family, community, nation, or the world. But only one is *dominus*, Lord, Jesus the Christ. [2]

Religious leaders may have more power to control groups than they realize.

Jesus entered this world as an infant, not at all in control. In the wake of threats to Jesus' life, Joseph and Mary took the child and fled to Egypt. Dorothee Soelle's *The Strength of the Weak* describes Christ's refusal to take control even of his own destiny, and to align himself with the poor, the powerless, and the vulnerable. [3] But, in a false sense of piety, we should not confuse Jesus' powerful love with weak resignation. Jesus was deliberate in walking into and through conflict. In prayerful discernment of the will of God, Jesus controlled when he would engage in conflict, with whom, and how. Even in the hands of powerful people he exercised control of himself in the midst of conflict.

The disciples of Christ also faced much conflict. Immediately after the Resurrection the chief priests assembled with the elders and devised a plan to bribe the Roman soldiers to say the disciples stole the body from the grave when the soldiers were asleep (Matt. 28:11-15). The Holy Spirit at Pentecost (Acts 2) empowered "all who were together" to speak in the languages of those assembled from diverse regions. Even so, people sneered (v. 13). Throughout Acts and the Epistles we see the young church facing every imaginable type of conflict. We may wonder why the Holy Spirit did not control things in the early church more closely. Major church councils throughout history have been convened because of conflict. Church creeds were written in response to conflict.

Christians have an amazing propensity to engage in conflict. Many times the church has sought to control its people. The historic and global church has faced forces that have tried to control Christian people. We wonder, "What is the nature of the church? How much control do Christian leaders have or should they have?"

Relinquishing Control

Sister Marie Augusta Neal in her writings described a theology of relinquishment. Freed from needing to hoard power or lord it over others, we can lead with open hands, sharing power for the sake of conflict resolution.[4] Celia Hahn writes about maintaining one's leadership role while relinquishing control.[5] If God is in control, I do not need to desperately cling to control. Nor do I need to fear things getting out of control—at least never out of the hands of God. My own need to control may be a sign of my unbelief. I can exercise responsible leadership by relinquishing my tight grip on people and their gifts. As Barbara Jordan, former congresswoman, author, and educator, said, "You cannot give another person power, but you can allow them to take it."[6]

In dealing with conflict, one can relinquish control for a specific purpose, time, or task. That is quite different from abandoning people or abdicating one's office in the midst of conflict in the community. One relinquishes control by giving up overly managing other people's lives. As people take control of making their own decisions, amazing things can happen. They begin to take responsibility for their own conflicts and for finding ways to settle differences. One may most helpfully respond to conflict through control by retaining one's responsibility and sharing some of one's authority. A wise person knows when to be in charge and when to relinquish some power.[7]

One more thing needs to be said here. Pastors need to relinquish control when they leave a church.[8] Much damage has been done by pastors who, after they have left a congregation, come back to "solve a problem." Although well-meaning, they often cause more divisions, and difficulties for the new pastor. They become yet another player in a heated struggle for control. When you leave, leave: relinquish your role.

Being Controlled by Control

The power to control is seductive. We know of leaders of faith communities, organizations, corporations, and nations whose power has grown to the extent that they have seemingly ultimate control over all decisions in the lives of people. One can exercise limited control in just ways so that differences can be resolved. One can also exercise control in ways that disable people from knowing their own minds and using their own gifts. What happens when the ability to control moves into the *need* to control?

Those who live in the United States of America need to seriously engage the question of what it means to live in a nation that at this time in history seemingly has the power to exercise influence all over the world. One cannot and should not try to completely or forever control other nations. What is the role of leadership based on power? What are the dangers? Strong, healthy leadership needs to be separated from the need for power.

Likewise, when you, as leader (perhaps without even knowing how much power you have), are able to exercise control in situations of conflict, what are the opportunities and the dangers of using control? Control can be a form of manipulation. Occasionally the person attempting to control a situation is trying to cover up their ignorance of the larger system. Such a person, feeling less and less confident, will have to exercise more and more control. Excessive control is rarely effective.

Collaborating on Control

To control sounds like the very opposite of to collaborate. But, when one understands the responsibility of authority and the role of relinquishment, one can choose control as a response to conflict, exercising leadership in a conflict situation in collaborative ways. People in the conflicted group can agree to, or at least allow, a leader to take control of a situation. Such agreement, freely given, is itself collaboration.

Even though we may think we can take control without another's consent, such control is an illusion. If people are being controlled against their will, the conflict will not go away, just underground. Some people will rebel, and sabotage the leader. Other people, not able to resist, will simply quit; yet others may literally become sick. Their alternatives may be restricted, but God's Spirit will not be squelched. However, when people express confidence in their leader, they effectively collaborate with that leader who is exercising authority in a healthy manner. Pastors need to know when to use control as the appropriate response to conflict.

Control as a Response to Conflict

When to Take Control

- When conflict is escalating to a point that safety is a significant issue

- When tempers are running high and things are becoming chaotic
- When people's physical, mental, or emotional health is threatened
- When through taking control early on, unnecessary conflict can be avoided
- When control will reshape the conflict so that more people will be able to exercise their voices
- When reshaping the agenda to move a stalled meeting off dead center
- When there is a leadership vacuum and a negative force is taking hold
- When deadlines are looming and strong leadership is needed
- When there is a need to help people be accountable to commitments and choices
- When one has enough power *to* take control (Trying to exercise control without power has negative consequences for oneself and for the group.)
- When setting boundaries and providing direction

When to Relinquish Control

- When being in control dampens people's spirits and inhibits their gifts
- When people have skills themselves to see the conflict through
- When new leadership is emerging
- When yielding to another's expertise
- When everyone is merely being quiet and listening only to you
- When people have become dependent on you to make decisions for them
- When keeping control causes a conflict to broaden underground
- When controlling a meeting keeps the truth from coming out
- When one's own opinions and investment in the issues are too strong

- When one's focus is no longer on the best interest of the community
- When, after setting a trustworthy environment, one can let go of needing to determine, or even influence, the outcome

What are other situations where taking control was necessary and positive? What are other experiences you have had when the leader helpfully relinquished control and by so doing empowered the group?

What or Whom Are You Controlling?

Being in Control of People

The question arises, *Can a person actually control people?* Even so, should one? There are occasions when a leader will need to step in to stop people from hurting themselves or others. But exercising control over people in a given situation should not extend to the control of other aspects of their life. How do people interpret such control? What ramifications does it have? Should a leader ever dismiss someone from a class or church meeting?

Sometimes leaders surrender too much control. For example, if a pastor abdicates being in control of a wedding rehearsal, a family member or florist or photographer may take over, causing all sorts of problems. Or, when tempers flare on a task force and the pastor backs away from dealing with the warring parties, someone will step in to deal with the situation and it may not be the right person.

Likewise, having a vacuum of leadership at a meeting can drive people crazy.[9] The meeting goes nowhere. The group can't decide on a direction and people just spin their wheels. A leader will help by taking charge of the group, focusing their attention and facilitating process. Then, once they are on track, he or she can gradually relinquish that control so people can make difficult decisions collaboratively.

People can benefit from knowing to whom they can turn. That may be as simple as being able to recognize the role an existing leader is going to play in the conflict. A leader stepping up to take control helps people know that they are going to address a conflict and that there will be clarity rather than chaos. When young persons or persons new to a role do not yet have the skill to lead a group through conflict, they may be given limited authority. They then have a safety net of having someone else ultimately in charge while they grow into their new role. They will benefit from a mentor who helps them reflect on how things are going and what they might try next time.

Being in charge of people takes courage, boldness, wisdom, restraint, and patience. Collaborative control is based on authority, trust, and accountability.

Providing Control for the Agenda

Religious leaders may have more power to control groups than they realize. A leader can stack the deck, either through appointments to a committee or through setting the agenda as to what difficult issues a group will deliberate. A wise leader will share power by disseminating information. A prudent leader will guide a group through the amount of decision making they can helpfully make at a given time. And a good leader *will* exercise some control over an agenda to assure that justice is served in how conflicted issues come before the assembly. If he or she does so without using intimidation, the group will be able to change the agenda if they feel they are ready to move at a different pace through conflict, or in a different direction.

But how do you helpfully use control when you are not the leader? Perhaps you are a religious leader of the faith community but not chairing a particular board, and the group frequently becomes mired in controversy. One way to use control is to meet with the chair between meetings to talk about what happened and to set the next agenda. Do preparatory work together; lay the groundwork. Then the chair will know you are a partner, that you trust him or her and will be there to assist in keeping order. This is much better than taking over, directly or indirectly, within a meeting.

A person who does not hold any office can still exercise control by asking appropriate, respectful, specific questions and thereby refocusing discussion. While not directly taking control by "seizing the microphone," one might ask, "How might we facilitate the resolution of this?" or "How can we work toward consensus?" Many times a gentle nudge helps support a meek leader.

Controlling Means and Methods

Pastors can use their authority to decide (or together with others help decide) what methods a group might use to deal with conflict. When people are frustrated, they may raise their voices, refusing to listen to one another or resorting to name-calling. Or, to avoid conflict, they may get themselves bogged down in extraneous details. At that point—or, better yet, before that point—one can set the ground rules. A leader can deliberately stop some unhelpful means of communication by simply taking control of the process: "We are not going to continue raising our voices and interrupting one another. We are going to take turns speaking, and this is how that is going to happen...." One can take control quietly, but that is not to be confused with only "sort of" taking control.

We should not control decisions, but we can use appropriate authority to control the means people will use to make those decisions. We cannot control people's viewpoints, but we can make sure that methods are congruent with mission. We should not use overt or covert control to assure a certain outcome, but we can use an authoritative voice to keep purposes before the group and processes open.

People want to be empowered to deliberate. One can tell when there is vital, engaging debate. Likewise, one can tell when a group has become entangled in amendments to amendments or when it has grown tired and wants to come to a consensus (or vote, if necessary). Through a rhythm of openness and drawing the group back, one guides the process. Groups, especially when they have grown cranky through conflict, need and appreciate such calm control of the means toward collaborative deliberation over difficult issues.

Controlling the Environment

I believe it is not only the right but also the responsibility of leaders to use their authority to set and maintain a trustworthy arena where differences can emerge, voices can be heard, issues explored, and conflict resolved. [10] If a leader does not do so, it will be much harder for members of the group to establish and maintain such an environment. When leaders value and invest their power and authority in carefully establishing this environment, the group will help maintain and, at subsequent meetings, reestablish this place where things are "under control."

A trustworthy environment is not a closed environment. Some people might worry that a set agenda and chosen methods might lead to a scripted meeting. That could be the result: those in charge exercising power for a predetermined outcome to the conflict. But, paradoxically, a well-set environment can become the most open. With a framework safely in place, people can feel safe enough to be honest and open. When leaders use their legitimate power to establish an environment where all parties to the conflict have a place and equal voice at the table, justice will be served by the full range of opinions being expressed. [11]

Groups appreciate calm control of the means toward collaborative deliberation over difficult issues.

When leaders take time to know the people and caringly control a healthy environment, they will not need to use loud voices or threats to control behavior.

By setting and maintaining an ongoing safe, healthy, trustworthy environment, faith communities are more able to deal with conflicts as part of their regular life together. This is control exercised—and received collaboratively—routinely as part of life together. This helps maintain a "disciplined" community of disciples able to deal with the challenges of differences.

Personal Reflection
Consider one area of responsibility where you might need to exercise *more* control. How might that be helpful in stopping unhealthy conflict? How might that contribute to creating and maintaining a healthy environment in which to deal with conflict?

Collegial Conversation
If by now you as colleagues know one another well and trust one another, play a game. Take turns taking control through the power of words or actions. (You might use a ball or a water bottle. You might try to out-talk one another. You might try to take control through speaking very softly.) See how you react. Talk about what you learned about yourself, about your colleagues.

Notes

1. See Daniel L. Olson, "The Well-being of Individuals and the Health of the Community," in Norma Cook Everist, ed., *The Difficult But Indispensable Church* (Minneapolis: Fortress Press, 2002), pp. 33-34. Olson explores how the loss of primary control is harmful to the individual, but, having lost that control, the individual's exercise of secondary control strategies is harmful to communities. Using the biblical mandate of stewardship, Olson says that stewards have been put "in charge." He recommends that people relinquish the need to be in control in favor of taking charge of that for which they have responsibility (pp. 40-41).

2. Genesis 1–3 has been interpreted many ways in regard to the relationship of human beings to the rest of creation.

3. See Dorothee Soelle, *The Strength of the Weak* (Philadelphia: Westminster Press, 1984).

4. See Marie Augusta Neal, *A Socio-theology of Letting Go* (New York: Paulist Press, 1977).

5. See Celia Allison Hahn, *Growing in Authority, Relinquishing Control* (Bethesda, Md.: Alban, 1994).

6. Barbara Jordan addressing the Lutheran Human Relations Association annual meeting at Valparaiso University, Valparaiso, Indiana, June 1964.

7. Hahn, *Growing in Authority, Relinquishing Control*, p. 30. Hahn views control negatively, making the case that integrated authority honors the freedom of others.

8. Ibid., pp. 164-65. Hahn says that within the congregation and beyond, church leaders ought to view their role as interim and their authority as temporary.

9. During the large power outage in the parts of the Midwestern and Eastern United States and Canada, 14 August 2003, Mayor Kwame Kilpatrick of Detroit praised his city's emergency readiness team, saying they may have had a power vacuum but not a leadership vacuum.

10. See chapter 2, "Creating Effective Learning Environments to Be Different Together," in Norma Cook Everist, *The Church as Learning Community* (Nashville: Abingdon Press, 2002), pp. 61-102.

11. I was completing the third draft of this manuscript while attending a national church body assembly. At the first session the presiding bishop took great care and time to make sure not only that each of the more than one thousand delegates had information, but that they understood and felt comfortable with the procedures that would be used at the week-long convention. Microphones and electronic voting machines were working; there would also be a clear balance of those speaking for and against an issue. The leader set an environment that was clear and comfortable, formal enough for rules to serve, and open enough for new voices to speak. He openly stated that this was to assure that power would not be in the hands of only a few. Midway through the week he took time to clarify procedures again. He was clearly in control of the environment of the assembly; the healthy control engendered trust. They were able to deal with controversial issues.

CHAPTER TEN

ACCOMMODATION

T hat's OK. I don't mind. We'll do it your way."
"How nice of you to be accommodating."
That exchange between coworkers or committee members could be followed by adding, "Next time we'll go with your choice."

Or, it could be followed by a whole string of the same outcomes to disagreement, either spoken or unspoken, and finally by the assumption that it's always OK to do it "your way."

The former is a healthy dance of partnership, a collaborative way of mutual accommodation, often through simply taking turns. The latter is a pattern of dominance and submission, reinforced again and again until the one who "gives in" loses a sense of the worth of his or her ideas and abilities, and finally a loss of a sense of self. [1] Likewise, the one who always gets his or her way reinforces a posture of privilege and superiority.

The Faces and Postures of Accommodation

Do you ever find yourself accommodating? What does accommodation sound like to you? What does it look like?

Do you routinely expect certain people or groups of people to accommodate to you? What do you believe status of age, gender, office, economic class, and education have to do with accommodation?

One sees accommodation when one sees people making room for others' views while maintaining their own integrity.

One can accommodate willingly or begrudgingly. Those expressions of accommodation (whether they show on the face or not) will look very different. One may appear to be accommodating to other voices in the group, but is merely waiting to get the last word. (Using silence and position as power.)

To accommodate is more than merely yielding, for that looks as if we don't care. Genuine accommodation is a gracious act that honors other persons and gives way. In so doing we may meet someone at the point of his or her deepest need, and do more than we might have known.

Hospitality

Accommodation might simply look like hospitality. To be hospitable is to make room for the other. "I'm going to accommodate you," means to make space for the other's opinions, ideas, and for their very being. It includes treating people as treasured guests, tending their needs, making their stay comfortable. Accommodation, while seeming weak, can be a very strong response to conflict. Accommodation requires thoughtfulness, self-control, courtesy (a word not used much anymore in our society), and a willingness to listen and to learn.

But at first glance one may sense a power imbalance in the response of accommodation. Some worry that to accommodate is to go "one down." They fear losing respect. On the other side of the power imbalance, being accommodating or hospitable could be interpreted as being paternalistic or maternalistic. [2] The one with the most resources, the most "rooms," makes space for the outsider, the other. That is why it is important that we consider the collaborative approach of mutual hospitality. [3] People make room for one another. Even though they are different in ability, resources, strength, or position, they all have something to give: respect and dignity. [4] And they all have something to let go of: their own need to cling to personal preferences.

124

To be hospitable is not to relinquish totally one's place of dwelling, whether that is one's office space, one's home, or one's personhood. We make room for the other, but we do not abandon our opinions and convictions. I will welcome you into my home but I will not become the door- mat. I will make space for your ideas, listen respectfully to even your strongest convictions, but I will not let your voice drown out my own. I will hold on to my own beliefs while making room for yours. This is a challenging way to think about dealing with con- flict. We not only make space for those of opposing views, but we move into that space together.

> *In the collaborative approach of mutual accommodation, people make room for one another.*

Making Room for All

This approach has consequences. What if you move into my space and we find there is not room for both of us? What if the community has such a wide range of values and viewpoints that it would be difficult to accommodate all of them? What if I am accommodating and you take advantage of the situation? Might I not fear that you will take over? What if we discover our con- flicting views are mutually exclusive? What do we do then? (We might consider the response in the next chapter.) Even more common in church conflict at the congregation and broader church level is that often one party's sphere is so defined as to make impossible the inclusion of the other's beliefs, values, mis- sion, or ministry. In that case, mutual accommodation remains merely a nice idea. How sad and how real!

In the broader society, we speak of "public accommodations." We work for justice to make sure that public spaces—such as restau- rants, golf courses, and government agencies—are open to all. To accommodate by hospitably opening up such places for a wide variety of different backgrounds and races, both genders, and the full range of political views is a challenge. Providing an open trustworthy environment is an essential part of hospitality. Private meetings, whether they are a small group meeting behind the pastor's back or an exclusive group of church insiders, are an all too familiar way of dealing with conflict. People wield power in unjust ways for their own welfare at the expense of the others. To truly be hospitable to all, to accommodate publicly, makes room for all people and all opinions—and potentially for a just resolution to the conflict.

Jesus

Mary and Joseph met an inhospitable Bethlehem when Jesus was about to be born. Shortly after Jesus' birth, King Herod was unable to accommodate the presence of the potential threat to his power.

Jesus' entire life and ministry were met with an inhospitable response. People were threatened by his teachings and his ministry. And yet Jesus was hospitable to all whom he met. He accommodated himself to their claims on his time. He accommodated himself to their questions and their needs—yet not entirely so. He knew when he needed to go apart to pray. He knew when he needed to rest. He knew when it was time to move on to the next town.

Jesus, the Christ, could not accommodate to the legalistic views of religious authorities. He would not accommodate to the exclusion of children, women, people who were poor, or outcasts. Jesus' refusal to accommodate to judgmental attitudes and injustice was rooted in his radical hospitality. Through prayer, he continually discerned the will of the One who had sent him. Jesus did not seek conflict or the cross. But he became accommodating to the will of God. Through such radical accommodation has come salvation. Christ's radical hospitality of unconditional acceptance of all (redemption) has put an end to strife (conflict). Living in the forgiveness of sins opens up the possibility of resolution of our human conflicts.

The power of God's grace challenges and empowers human beings toward reconciliation. No matter how deep the conflict, the Holy Spirit creates new ways for us to be the church together, always calling us to open our doors to those for whom we would have no room.

Discipleship

"Do not be conformed to this world." One could conclude that the way of discipleship is decidedly not to accommodate. Some Christians would remind people that to accommodate is to give in to Satan, secularism, or the claims of other religions. Certainly the call to disciples is a call to commitment to Christ. This call takes one away from the world, with its false hopes and promises. But just as the call to discipleship calls us away from the world's ways of wielding power, so, too, Christ sends us right back into the world. We are called to live and work beside those very different from ourselves and to make room for them with their varied beliefs.

To be disciples of Christ is to take on the mind of Christ (Philippians 2:5-11). We are called into community to be disciples (plural). Thus, we are not called to give in to the dominating influence of another. (That applies *inside* the church as well as in the world.) Nor are we to expect another to always accommodate to us or to the dominant group in the church (even to the *majority*). By grace we are being conformed to the image of Christ. In seeking the will of God, we as members of a Christian community accommodate to Christ in accommodating to one another.

Mutual Accommodation as a Lifestyle of Discipleship

"All well and good," you say. "We believe in a reconciling God. But in the real world things don't go that way." No, they do not. Although Jesus' death and resurrection have been accomplished for all time and for all peoples, human beings live in the world where conflict is still all too common. Because jealousy, manipulation, dissension, and war are so much the fabric of human relationships, we have a tendency to disconnect Christian beliefs from life together. We have a five-minute devotion at the beginning of a church council meeting and then move right into a major fight over the church budget. So, how do we connect being disciples with handling our conflicts? How do we collaborate as a community of disciples in mutual accommodation?[5] How do we know when it is wise to accommodate and when it is not?

The Use of Accommodation

When to Accommodate

- When it is the gracious thing to do
- When making space for new people in the group
- When the relationship is currently more important than the outcome
- When the other party has accommodated recently
- When you can accommodate another's preferences without sacrificing your own core convictions
- When you have the time, resources, and capacity to do so
- When there is the possibility of injury to someone if you do not
- When someone has been feeling left out and accommodating to their suggestion will help them feel more a part of the group
- When teamwork is important and taking turns needs to be demonstrated
- When to do so serves a larger purpose
- When it will help you and the group be open to new views and deeper relationships
- When by doing so, an environment of reciprocity is encouraged

When Not to Accommodate

- When core values would be compromised
- When you or others may lose self-respect
- When it is the easy way out
- When it is done merely to "be nice"
- When it is done only to score points
- When repeatedly accommodating results in power within the group remaining with the same person or clique
- When you accommodate only because you don't have information and are afraid to ask

- When you are accommodating on behalf of another without their consent
- When you are being emotionally manipulated into believing you ought to accommodate
- When you have been accommodating regularly to a person or group
- When you are being taken advantage of
- When you do so at risk to your own health or well-being

Red Flags

Lest you picture accommodation in the midst of conflict as everyone tiptoeing around issues ("You go first." "No, you go first."), let's point out some red flags in the use of accommodation that you may have already thought of.

1. A community may be merely being polite and not genuinely accommodating at all. Unwilling accommodation is not healthy. The issues will resurface in some other form. A quick accommodation as a last-ditch effort may seem like a way to end the contention, but resentment may result. Or the pretense of accommodation may be a way for some to exit the community altogether. Genuinely making space for one another needs to be a vibrant way to keep people engaged. [6]

2. Accommodation can take place without our knowing it. Those in authority need to be careful that people are not deferring simply because of office, position, or longevity. An entire community may just assume newcomers will fit in to their established ways of being or dealing with conflict. We can help make sure that doesn't happen by continuing to affirm and use people's gifts and by drawing out people's opinions.

3. When people have broken relationships, making room for one another seems fragile, uneasy. Perhaps a pattern has developed of some people never accommodating. Others risk being taken advantage of or being deeply hurt. But accommodation, freely offered, can be a helpful way to reestablish relationships, particularly if we trust that Christ has borne our brokenness and that the Spirit can work

within even the bitterest conflict. At some deep level of faith the estranged parties know they can benefit from mutual hospitality. Accommodation in strained relationships means not giving up, or just giving in, but opening up to one another and new possibilities.

4. Nonverbal communication can signal that a person is not freely accommodating. Eye rolling may show contempt or scorn. Arms folded across the chest may indicate that the person is "giving in" this time but may retaliate when given a chance. Sighing can indicate exasperation, impatience, or futility—none of which is healthy accommodation.

5. We may be tempted to accommodate to those in authority just because of their position. (If a person is exercising that kind of authority, he or she is using inappropriate control.) Do not accommodate to those in authority just because you think they must know better than you. You can respect authority and hear their wisdom, but no one has total knowledge. Know yourself. Even if it seems the "safer" thing to do to give way automatically, ask yourself, "Do they really have ultimate control?" We can raise questions, seek a broader range of advice, explore options, and make room for the Spirit. Accommodation needs to be a chosen response to conflict, and done freely.

Using a Combination of Response Styles

As we have moved through the various responses to conflict, it is common to note that we rarely use just one response in a conflict, especially in considering accommodation. We see various combinations emerging. Accommodation can even be a way to *avoid* conflict. That can be negative, but if avoidance for a time *is* the appropriate response (see chapter 6), taking time and opportunity to accommodate others for the sake of strengthening relationships can be a helpful strategy.

A youth director taking young people on a trip to a regional youth gathering faces the daily deluge of questions and opinions about where the group is going to stop for lunch, and how much time should be given for "free time," and what activities are outside the bounds of the covenant the group made with one another when they began the trip. The youth director has to consider the delicate balance between accommodation and *confrontation*. A rhythm of the two can be a helpful combined strategy to address the conflicts that simply will arise when a group spends that much time together for a week.

A program director at a rehabilitation facility said that her job involves confrontation most every day. They are helpful confrontations because they are purposeful. In adopting a hospitable presence, she has discovered fewer hidden agendas than she might have feared. With an openness of accommodation, more helpful *confrontation* can occur. This results in an energized sense of hope for more healthy ways to live in community.

A pastor may need to take *control* of a situation where some people are always giving in to the will of the powerful. By giving leadership to changing the environment, the group might eventually move to more mutual accommodation as a way to deal with their conflicts.

Accommodation may be a good first step toward *compromise* (which we will address in the next chapter). It can help develop relationships by people stating their needs and even their preferences. When accommodation is genuine, compromise will be possible.

Communication Strategies

In order for mutual accommodation to be more than a nice term on paper, here are some specific strategies:

- When a group is heading toward gridlock, adopt a method of taking turns expressing desires and needs. Make sure the group knows the difference between the two.
- Use methods of going around the table so that everyone speaks, thereby drawing out silent voices and quieting dominating ones. Practice asking people's opinions and accommodating to a shy person's idea. (You may wish to give people time to write their responses first. Some people are more confident in sharing this way.)
- Model accommodation on small, nonagenda-related issues so that people begin to trust that they can work toward mutual accommodation.

- When difficulties arise, try saying, "In order for this conflict to be resolved, what do you need from me? May I tell you what I need from you?"
- Determine together who needs more to be accommodated *this time*.
- Refrain from placing demands on one another. Allow one another freedom to offer the hospitality of accommodation.
- When there is doubt, try saying, "I think your solution is worth considering, but let's see what others have to say." Accommodation may take some time to work out.
- When there is skepticism, try saying, "I see that this is very important to you. Let's imagine what taking it in that direction might look like." Help people see the consequences of the group's accommodation to their wishes.
- When differences are wide: "Your approach is really different from mine. I'll go along with it, but I know I may become anxious at times." A good response: "It helps me understand your anxiety. Please tell me when this path becomes difficult for you."
- When self-esteem is at risk: "I am not sure that what I am asking for is worth the price of losing your voice in the matter."
- Try accommodation to time, but not to mission: "Your family time is of higher priority than a second meeting right now. We can look at a later reschedule date."
- When one person is accommodating more often than others: "I'll go along with the decision, but it feels like I'm the one who is accommodating a lot lately. Does it seem that way to you?"
- When a predecessor was less accommodating to people's creativity than you want to be: "It seems like you are tentative in saying your preferences. I wonder how we might change that."

Personal Reflection

Spend some time in personal prayer and reflection. Write in a journal if that is helpful. Do I believe I am more accommodating than I need to be or that is healthy for me and my relationships?

What have been the consequences of that? Honestly, do people accommodate to me more than I may realize? How might I change either of these postures so that I can be a more effective partner in resolving conflict?

Collegial Conversation

On the way toward collaborative mutual accommodation, some of us will need to unlearn ways of engaging in conflict and learn new ways. Try this as a staff or small group:

Make up an inconsequential situation rather than a current real conflict. For example: You are going out to eat together and need to select a restaurant. You each have a distinct preference. On a scale of one to ten, decide how accommodating you usually are in the midst of conflict. Play out this scenario according to your usual style. Exaggerate your roles for fun, if you wish.

What did you notice about the way the scenario went? Have each person in turn say how they felt. What assumptions about other people and their opinions were being made? Allow opportunity for people to ask questions of one another as to what they did and why.

Play out the scenario again, but this time reverse roles—have the one who is lowest on the accommodation scale be the most accommodating, and so forth. How did the scenario go this time? What did you learn about yourself? About others? How might each of you take on attributes of healthy mutual accommodation?

Notes

1. Marshall Shelley, ed., *Leading Your Church Through Conflict and Reconciliation* (Minneapolis: Bethany, 1997), pp. 179-80. The author tends toward seeing accommodation as being merely "cuddly." For those who believe relationships are always more important than issues, any disagreement will be bad. Extended "generosity" can lead one to finally quit a group.

2. See Ronald W. Richardson, *Creating a Healthier Church* (Minneapolis: Fortress Press, 1996). Richardson examines family systems theory and congregational life. He looks at unbalanced systems, birth order, and seeing the congregation as an emotional system. This can be helpful in determining when power is being abused in unhealthy accommodation.

3. See Donald E. Messer, *A Conspiracy of Goodness: Contemporary Images of Christian Mission* (Nashville: Abingdon Press, 1992). In chapter 5 (pp. 91-108), Messer describes "a collegiality of bridge builders." The image of a bridge helpfully shows what mutual accommodation could look like in a congregation.

4. See the classic work by Parker Palmer, *The Company of Strangers* (New York: Crossroad, 1981). Palmer's thesis is that one should not try too soon to turn the stranger into friend, but to hospitably welcome that which is different into the relationship.

5. See Evelyn Eaton Whitehead and James D. Whitehead, *Community of Faith: Crafting Christian Communities Today* (Mystic, Conn.: Twenty-Third Publications, 1992). The work of creating hospitable places for mutual accommodation may be central to ministry in communities of faith.

6. Joyce L. Hocker and William W. Wilmot, *Interpersonal Conflict*, 6th ed. (Boston: McGraw-Hill, 2001), pp. 158-60. "The accommodating person may think that he or she is serving the good of the group, family, or team by giving in, sacrificing, or stepping aside. Sometimes this is true; often, however, the accommodator could better serve the needs of the larger group by staying engaged longer" (p. 158).

COMPROMISE

You're going to have to compromise!" That doesn't sound very promising. It sounds more like a threat than a promise. Likewise, "being compromised" sounds invasive. Whereas compromise might appear to be a fair way to resolve conflict, to many of us this response may not seem very appealing.

To compromise requires going halfway. That may be going halfway toward meeting the other whose views we oppose. Does compromise mean I can win only halfway? Doesn't it also mean rather than losing totally, I lose only one half?

Compromise means ending a stalemate, reaching an agreement. That in itself brings a sigh of relief. The compromise may be the best one can do. The alternative, to fail to reach a solution all parties can agree to, continues strife, risks conflict escalation, and halts collaborative work. The cost of not compromising can be high—in productivity, time, and relationships. The longer two parties stay locked in disagreement, the further apart they may drift. Congregations may not just drift apart, but rupture.

"To be compromised" is passive. "To compromise" is active.

Whereas compromise offers a way for all to have an equal role in solution to conflict, some people may be "more equal than others." Compromise can be a game that requires mental and linguistic agility. Some of us

135

have developed such skill. Others feel lost from the start. Those who know how to play the game refuse to compromise until the very last minute so that they can win as much as possible. Compromise is promising, but also risky.

Compromise is moderately assertive and moderately cooperative. It is dependent upon sharing power, and this is a radical concept in cultures that for generations have been based on domination and submission. [1] If one is seen as having very little power in a situation, the more powerful finds no compelling reason to compromise. Likewise, the one with less power will welcome compromise little more than competition. Although compromise might be likened to collaboration (which we will explore in the next chapter), compromise differs in that although it takes less work, it requires trade-offs. People give a little and get a little, often depending upon how far apart they are when they begin. [2] Compromise is rarely the first choice when people face conflict, but is a daily part of life and is regarded positively in this society. [3]

Compromise: To Promise With

At the heart of compromise is "to make promises with." In this light, it can be a collaborative response to conflict. It can be the most direct route to a peaceful resolution of a conflict. We need people with skill to serve as counselors and mediators to help estranged parties come to a peaceful settlement in which neither has to totally lose. Mutual promise making is heartening. Mutual promise *keeping* is even better!

God's Uncompromising Love

God did not compromise in creating a wonderfully diverse and beautiful world. Neither did God compromise with the powers of sin and death! There was no bargaining, no halfway measure, when Jesus Christ went to the cross and was raised from the dead in order that human beings might be reconciled with God and one another forever. God is a God of covenant faithfulness and unconditional love. No conditions. Because of that we are able to be enfolded in God's gracious love and to be free to live in the promises of God.

No doubt about it, we continue to break the promises we make with one another. In continuing conflict, we drive one another to the breaking point. We break promising institutions, including the church. We are broken within. But we live in the promise—the reality—of God's uncompromising love. To compromise means first of all to forgive one another, to offer one another the absolution of Christ. *Com-promise* (living together in the promise) and *for-giveness* (the empathic journey together into a new life of compassion and love) go together. Compromise is not easy. We will make promises and break them. Through it all, God's covenant faithfulness surrounds us all, creating the groundwork and empowering us to live in community as the Body of Christ. As we gather at the Lord's Table, sharing bread and wine, we are strengthened for living together in the promises of God in order to freely compromise.

> *We live in the promise—the reality—of God's uncompromising love.*

There are many stories or themes in the Bible that convey God's promises. Here are only some:

- God's promise to Noah
- God's promise to Abraham and Sarah
- God's covenant with Israel
- Jesus' promises to the disciples
- Promises about the reign of God
- The promise to wait for the Holy Spirit

Freed from Being Compromised in Order to Freely Compromise

Have you ever felt compromised? Used for someone else's purposes? What was that like? What did that mean? What connotations does that phrase have for you?

We were not created in order to be compromised, either by God or by other people. A result of the human problem of sin is our dealing with conflict by either trying to get the upper hand and compromising another's position, or by going "one down" and giving in, being compromised.

Signs of Compromise

Negative Signs

- When a person is feeling trapped by having to go along with a decision
- When people are being forced to give up something
- When people feel belittled or humiliated, or have little control in the process
- When people come to the table with a long list of nonnegotiables
- When people paint themselves into a corner with ultimatums or limited choices
- When there are deeper issues that need to be addressed before a true compromise can be reached

Positive Signs

"To be compromised" is passive. "To compromise" is active. Compromise can be positive when all involved feel empowered to live through the conflict to a new way of living in community.

Mutual accommodation (see chapter 10) is a first step toward fruitful compromise. There are some ways to know when compromise is possible and how it can be positive.

- When all parties engage in the compromise process freely
- When compromise has the potential of bringing people together on neutral ground
- When the relationship has been established to the point that people know they can approach compromise with zeal
- When all parties are feeling that their ideas, desires, and gifts are being shared
- When people are being creative in possible new options
- When people begin to understand one another's needs and points of view through the very process of compromise

By saying, "Let's compromise so that we can move to a place where we both can work on this project together," there can be a growing benefit to the relationship as well as to the substance of the compromise. In the process of compromise it is important for people to have the opportunity of prioritizing, describing on a continuum what for them is more important to least important. The group may come to see that they can compromise their individual ambitions without compromising on the safety, welfare, or integrity of the community. Clearly compromise is a "middle ground" that can result from good-faith efforts. When seen as the cup "half full," it can produce effective results.

Varieties of Compromise

There is give-and-take in compromise. The central issue may not be *when* and *when not* to compromise (compromise is always useful when people disagree), but on *what* and on *what not* to compromise. The essence of compromise means we may not obtain all the things we had desired in order to attain a peaceful outcome. In matters of religion, compromise could be seen as a form of unfaithfulness. But compromise is not so much about changing what one holds dear (except positively changing by coming to new understandings) as about finding a solution for what troubles a faith community.[4] Looking back at the types of conflict (see chapter 2), we can discover ways to compromise. When assessing a conflict:

1. You might conclude you cannot compromise on *facts (truth)* but can compromise on the meaning of *beliefs* about those facts, or at least allow for a variety of meanings.

Example: A congregation is engaged in a conflict over your preaching about the importance of the Ten Commandments. Some say that to reach new people the church should not emphasize them. After all, "People get upset with all those rules." Obviously, you cannot compromise about retaining the Ten Commandments—or choose only a few of the "easier" ones on which to preach and teach.[5] However, there is room for difference on the meaning of those commandments, especially among people at different stages of the life cycle. To a young child "you shall not steal" means to not take a cookie from the cookie jar if someone bigger than you is watching. Grade-school children talk about "being fair." Teenagers, now able to do abstract reasoning, will be able to consider sins of "omission" as well as sins of "commission." A young adult may become adamant about punishment for one person's wrongdoing. A person of middle years, who can now deal with paradox, may look at the larger issues of justice. A young adult may regard such a viewpoint as compromising. Meanwhile an older adult may begin to see "you shall not steal" in terms of leaving bequests for the next generation. People of different stages of faith in the same congregation will hold different "beliefs" about the same truth.

2. You might feel strongly that you cannot compromise on your basic *beliefs*, but can compromise on the *mission (goals)* you would be willing to pursue, at least at this particular time.

Example: An interfaith group is collaborating on plans for a Memorial Day service at the local cemetery. Your church has participated for many years. For some this holiday calls for rituals of intense national patriotism. For others this is a time to remember

people from all nations who have died in battle, and for commitment to renewed efforts toward global peace. For some this is a
time to witness only to belief in Jesus Christ. For other Christians,
who hold equally strong beliefs about Christ, the mission of this
day is for people of many faiths to be together in common com-
memoration. As a leader among leaders of other faith communities, you may need to compromise on your goal for all the activities
for that day while still holding on to your beliefs to which you will
give public voice. The group may compromise by having an address
rather than a sermon; a variety of people offering prayers rather
than one "inclusive" Christian prayer; and the group may need to
compromise on the number and placement of flags.

3. You might be willing to compromise on *values (worth)* as
long as you don't compromise on *ministry*.

Example: The congregation you serve seems stuck. They want
to have a church that meets their personal needs but resist any
effort to lead them into ministry in the community. You hold
that being a Christian necessarily means being engaged in ministry beyond the local church. In order to get through this bar-
rier, you may be willing to compromise what activity (e.g.,
volunteering at a nursing home, cleaning up the highway) of
ministry they take on. After all, you figure discipleship takes
many forms and can involve people holding very different values. Rather than debate the values (which could delay ministry
for years to come), you simply want to see the congregation
move into some kind of action. By collaboratively engaging in
ministry, they may act their way into a new way of believing.
They may lessen their conflict through shared service. As they
engage in ministry together, what they believe and value may
become not less, but more clear.

4. You feel strongly about the *way (means)* the church should
engage in *ministry*, and, in order to help a group move beyond
competing plans, you want to help them compromise on *goals*.

Example: The finance and evangelism committees are desperate
to accomplish their goal: to increase membership. You see a conflict
coming—probably between these committees. The finance committee wants to secure names of residents of a new affluent suburb and
particularly invite them to church. The evangelism committee has

asked for budget funds to offer prizes ("incentives") to new people who come to church and to those who invited them. You encourage the groups to compromise on the goals they have; you do not believe they should compromise on means. No matter what action plan each group adopts, the means cannot justify the ends. If the congregation is going to reach out to people with the good news, the evangelism strategy cannot bribe people to come to church. Even if there is substantial stress and increasing conflict over financial security, ministry must not be aimed only at potential "good" givers, but directed toward all. Your aim is to help increase their skill not only in welcoming, but also in inviting people to Jesus Christ.

5. You will not compromise on *values* and so you are willing to compromise on *facts*. This may sound odd. How can one compromise on facts, on the *truth*?

Example: The congregation is embroiled in debate about what happened a year ago on the youth camping trip (or women's retreat, anniversary planning committee, and so forth). People simply remember things differently. They viewed the same event through different eyes. One could spend needless energy trying to reconstruct the event. More important is to stop the name-calling. The congregation needs to move ahead toward a shared sense of worth and value in being the church. In so doing they will rekindle their valuing of one another as members of the Body of Christ. Too often we cling to "a mighty fortress is my truth," rather than "a mighty fortress is our God." It is possible for people to compromise on their "factual" accounts of the past so that they are not divided on their future call to discipleship.

There are other combinations of the types of conflict that could give room to compromise. What are some that come to mind from your own experience?

Guidance for Compromise

A business magazine advertisement headlines: "In business, you don't get what you deserve, you get what you negotiate," indicating that learning the skills of successful compromise ensures that you win. But if the essence of compromise is to live in the promises of the reconciling love of God, then personal winning is not our goal for compromise.

A *Judging Amy* television episode featured a divorced couple disagreeing on the schooling for their teenage daughter. After hearing from the parents, the school, and finally the daughter, Judge Gray made her ruling, which mandated family counseling and all parties meeting back in court in three months. The mother said, "I don't understand. Who won here?" Judge Amy Gray replied, "You all did. You just don't know it yet." Even when tough decisions have to be made, compromise can mean all win, even if we don't realize it at the time.

People in some relationships seem to be able to compromise easily and often. There seems to be a regular rhythm of making choices, letting go of choices, and coming to a mutually satisfactory compromise about how they are going to spend time together, work together, minister together. The relationship itself and the shared mission are more important than one's own particular opinion. The pair, or the team, or the entire faith community simply enjoy being together.

For others, coming to a compromise in a conflicted situation is bitterly difficult. Perhaps one or more of the participants simply doesn't like seeing themselves as a "compromiser." Perhaps the issues at stake seem so important that to even give an inch is unthinkable. Perhaps the people simply don't like one another very much. At such times they will benefit from guidance in learning to compromise. Who knows, the practice may become habit forming!

The following roles can be useful in facilitating compromise: [6]

A leader, *to help a group make and adhere to a covenant.*

For example, a youth group is taking a trip to a national youth gathering. Traveling in vans, they will be together for a total of ten days. The youth, their parents, and the adult counselors hold vastly differing expectations of life together during the trip. A leader can help them, together, design a covenant. Although one could call them rules, they could also be named "promises" that they make with one another. Having agreed on the consequences of not keeping those promises, they will be more willing to accept the consequences. They probably will live up to what might be an even more stringent covenant than rules merely provided *for* them. In this case, the covenant of "making promises with" is much stronger than simply "guidelines."

A **counselor,** *to help two people, a family, or a staff live a more promising life together.*

A ministerial leader within the faith community or a trained counselor or spiritual guide sets a safe environment where people can begin to trust one another (or reestablish the trust they may have once had but which they have lost). He or she explores what is contributing to the parties feeling uncomfortable or anxious. The counselor helps them really listen to one another's experiences, and how they feel they might be compromised. They work on the relationships through mutual accommodation, taking time to be ready to compromise on the issues of the conflict. This most likely will take more than one session. They may start with compromising on small things and work toward compromise on the more challenging differences. At each step of the way the counselor guides them so that the process of compromise is life-giving.

A **mediator,** *to set clear boundaries and a process for problem solving.*

A mediator can help two or more people compromise in conflict over issues or in relationships by helping them make a covenant on ground rules; identify self-interests; define differences; formulate win-win resolutions; and account to the larger faith community.[7] For example, the church council president serves as mediator when the trustees and the youth group are arguing over whether or not the church should be unlocked all day on Sunday. Compromise is elusive. (You can't "half" lock a door.) The mediator finds a safe, neutral place to talk and ask them why they hold their respective positions. The youth leaders' mission is to be open to community youth who come early or late to Sunday four o'clock youth events. The trustees are concerned about security. The council president helps them formulate a resolution that meets both their needs. The church doesn't need to be unlocked all day; the youth just don't have a key. The trustees agree to provide a key for a youth leader to open the church at 3:30 P.M. and lock it at 7:30 P.M. The mediator reports this to the council so that others understand why and when the church will be unlocked. One can think of more difficult problems to solve, but the role of mediator and process remain.

Personal Reflection

Recall some situations in which you were able to provide leadership to people in using compromise to settle a conflict. Were you more of a counselor? A mediator? A leader? In retrospect, what skills do you already have? What skills do you wish to continue to develop?

Collegial Conversation

Share some positive experiences with compromise. What, if anything, did you feel was irreparably lost? Only temporarily lost? What was gained, both in the relationship and in a breakthrough in the conflict?

Notes

1. Riane Eisler and David Loye, *The Partnership Way: New Tools for Living and Learning* (San Francisco: HarperSanFrancisco, 1990). This book helps people understand the history of domination, particularly in gender relationships, and helps develop new skills for shared power and partnership.

2. Speed Leas, *Discover Your Conflict Management Style* (Washington, D.C.: Alban, 1997), pp. 23-27. Leas calls this "bargaining."

3. Joyce L. Hocker and William W. Wilmot, *Interpersonal Conflict,* 6th ed. (Boston: McGraw-Hill, 2001), pp. 156-57.

4. Joseph Phelps, *More Light, Less Heat* (San Francisco: Jossey-Bass, 1999), pp. 13-14.

5. Note that we speak here about retaining the Ten Commandments in a religious body, not in public places.

6. These roles might be played by any number of different people. For example, a pastor might serve as leader, or as pastoral counselor or, if he or she is not involved in the controversy, as mediator. Other lay or professional people might play one of these roles in a specific situation.

7. Hugh F. Halverstadt, *Managing Church Conflict* (Louisville: Westminster John Knox, 1991), pp. 149-68. Halverstadt separates the task of "negotiation" (substantive issues) from "mediation" (relational issues) (pp. 150-51, 157-63).

CHAPTER   TWELVE

COLLABORATION

L abor is part of life. Collaboration is essential to life together in the church. Throughout this book we have been using "collaboration" in two ways: (1) as one of the seven specific responses to conflict and (2) as a basic way of "working together" in every aspect of dealing with conflict. Collaboration is both a means and a goal; a strategy and a sustainable environment. In each of the six other strategies, we have mentioned the collaborative aspect of the response. In this chapter we shall look more closely at collaboration as a specific response to conflict.

To collaborate means, "to work together." A second meaning is "to side with the invaders of one's country." To be a collaborator can even seem sinister. One is selling out, not only one's principles, but also one's compatriots. We shall not specifically address that meaning in this chapter, but could this very positive response to conflict also have some negative aspects?

Collaboration means work! And who wants that? Avoiding conflict or having the power to simply keep a situation controlled is much easier (at least so it seems). Some people's experiences with collaboration have been lopsided. A team may be assigned to work together, but one person puts in most of the time and effort. Likewise, collaboration should not be confused with triangulation—two or more people bonding by turning on a third.

Collaboration is work we do together, a high-energy style particularly suited to people in long-term relationships such as a faith community. [1] When collaboration becomes an ongoing approach, it can help prevent people from using destructive means to deal with conflict. [2] Positively it demonstrates that people can work together, thereby becoming a witness to life together in community. [3]

There are limitations to each of the seven responses to conflict. If collaboration is the only style used, one can become imprisoned to it. [4] If investment in the relationship is low, it may not be worth the time and energy. A person unwilling to share power may control through pseudocollaboration. And one person who wants to use avoidance or competition negatively can frustrate the intentions of those who wish to collaborate. [5] However, collaboration can be very effective when a group is committed to working toward a creative, integrative solution to conflict.

At its best, to collaborate means to enjoy working together; to welcome diversity; to grow from challenge; to feel the satisfaction of time well spent together; to become more than one could ever become alone; to have struggled together to come through a very difficult conflict, emerging on the other side with sweat still on the brow but with a warm handshake or embrace. To collaborate in the midst of conflict can be, in the end, satisfying work.

Remember and Imagine

Recollection

Close your eyes and let your mind travel back to memories of collaboration in the midst of conflict. Open your eyes and make some notes.

1. As a child, were you encouraged to or discouraged from handling your own conflicts? (Did adults keep the environment safe or not?) Recall a time—at home, in school, on the playground—when you worked together in the midst of conflict. What happened? How did you feel? What was your role? Who helped or hindered you reach a satisfying (or dissatisfying) end to conflict?

2. As an adult, what skills have you learned to work on conflict? Recall a job situation of working together to deal with conflict. What do

you remember about yourself in that situation? Recall a relationship that required (requires) real work to deal with the ongoing reality of conflict. What is at stake in working together? What are the costs? The joys?

Imagine

Close your eyes and imagine a collaborative relationship that you would desire. What might that look like?

1. In a shared ministry in a faith community: How might power be shared, even with different authority roles? What would it contribute to joyful fatigue? How would conflict be resolved?

2. In a family relationship: We have many differing roles in our close and extended families. They change over time. Some relationships involve almost continuous conflict. At other times we are caught up short by the eruption of conflict. What might a collaborative process of dealing with conflict in your family look like?

3. In a friendship: Imagine a friendship in which collaboration is so satisfying that it endures almost without effort. Even friendships, of course, will have their times of conflict. And unlike family, one can change one's friends. Imagine what a trusted collaborative friendship, which stays with you through all kinds of conflict, would look like.

Perhaps you have some of these collaborative relationships in your life now. Blessed are you!

Shared Reflections

John: Conflict doesn't have to be an angry kind of thing, full of dissension. I imagine something positive.

Katie: After a grueling conflict, I don't want the relationship merely returned to what it was; I want it new and different.

Jessie: Collaboration has a creative element, whereas compromise can be giving up on creative solutions too soon.

Darin: When a leader is merely pseudocollaborative, he or she retains the power—and the work. That's not collaboration. People going home, satisfied with the decision or not, will probably put their energies elsewhere next time.

Steve: Yes. There's a complexity to collaboration, an evolution to the process. There is potential for it being ruptured when people don't carry through on what they agree upon.

Hannah: Collaboration takes sustained commitment. It's not a matter of conflict happening and you fix it. The work must be intentional.

Darin: If collaboration means merely consulting people but not including their opinions in the decision, it makes people wonder why they came to the meeting at all.

Rose: I process verbally and others do not. We also need to collaborate on a decision to take a break from conversation for those who process quietly.

> *Collaboration is essential for life together in Christian community.*

Jessie: That's why we need a hospitable environment where conflict can occur and creative collaboration can happen.

Steve: The work takes time, but you are working out conflict together so you can eventually move on.

Consensus

Collaboration holds promise—and it takes time. It is not to be equated with unanimity. Rather it is a *climate* or, as we have been saying throughout this book, a trustworthy environment where all are informed, communication is open, and each person has fair opportunity to influence the outcome.

Collaboration takes many forms. One important approach to dealing with differences is to make decisions by consensus. Consensus emphasizes cooperation in sharing information and airing differences. It is time-consuming but avoids win-lose results.[6] Obviously voting can be collaborative and consensus seeking can be manipulative or merely pseudocollaborative. Human beings are capable of wrecking any system.

In a Small Group

Here is one model of consensus seeking: When a proposal is put on the floor, a participant may agree, disagree, pass, stand aside, or call for a time-out. If a participant agrees with the proposal, then it moves on to the next person. If a participant disagrees, then he or she is responsible for stating a new proposal or modifying the current one. Once this is done, the proposal again begins to move around the group.

When participants pass, they do so in order to think about their position or to hear what others have to say. The proposal will come back around again to them and they will have another opportunity to state whether they agree or disagree. When participants stand aside they are asking for a permanent pass because of a conflict of interest. This option is used for participants who do not want to block the process of decision making. Finally, a participant may ask for a time-out to call for more clarification. Each person has input. The group works toward a decision.[7]

When the Group Is Large

Here is a sample process for group decision by consensus:[8]

A. Identify the issue.
B. Discuss the issue allowing adequate participation.
C. Test the proposal for agreement.
   a. Yes—consensus is reached.
   b. No—consider alternative proposals to resolve differences.
D. Resolving dissension:
   a. Reach consensus on alternative proposal.
   b. Postpone decision, repeating steps A to C.
   c. Move to small groups for further discussion.
   d. Failing consensus, refer to bylaws of the constitution of the group.
E. Options for dissension:
   a. Voice objection, but allow consensus, standing behind the decision.
   b. Voice objection, but remove self from the action of the decision.
   c. Block consensus decision.

Whatever the specifics of dealing with differences through consensus seeking, participants need to pray together and to listen to the movement of the Spirit. They need to be responsible for expressing their own opinions and feelings, and for listening to the strengths in the opinions of those with whom they may be in conflict. People will need time not only to understand the issue, but also to know their own minds and hearts on the matter so that later they do not think they could have gotten their point of view across had the others only understood what they *really* had in mind.

During the discussion, the leader or a group member may request a test for the "sense" of the group. Together the group will need to search for common ground, even if they do not agree on everything, and not just quickly come to a compromise. The collaborative work of consensus seeking does not end with making one decision, but is an ongoing process of life together in community.

Further Conversation on Collaboration

Eileen: Consensus, or for that matter collaboration in general, will not offer a magic solution, but, when used consistently, people become more familiar and comfortable with it. Power used as control seems strong, but it takes little courage; the shared power of partnership is life-giving, if fragile. It needs constant tending of the relationship.

Beth: I'm weary. I've just met with a group for the fourth time, collaborating on some work that was due today. We hope to finish it tomorrow. I like my group members, but I am far from enamored with this piece of work. We are tired and have other things to do. I could whine about it, but I really just want to raise the not so pleasant aspect of collaboration: the time-and-energy-consuming part.

Katie: In a group project I sometimes work extra hard because I don't want to let the others down. I recognize the skills of others, but with our different styles of working together, in some situations it is easier just to do it myself. But you really can't solve a conflict among people all by yourself.

Annika: There's another negative aspect to being a collaborator, which may connect to the second meaning of the word. In codependency, the victim allows himself or herself to collaborate with rescuer and persecutor. However, once anyone of these people makes changes in this unhealthy collaboration, the triangle breaks down. It will probably result in conflict, but will no longer perpetuate an unhealthy relationship. Then, with counseling, there's a possibility of a converse model of interdependency.

Eileen: Triangulation, or simply scapegoating others *is* a problem. At a church where I served, the group, mired in contentious relationships, took awhile to trust me as someone who wanted to lead them into a new way of dealing with conflict. They worried that I had some preconceived decision up my sleeve. Follow-through of mutual accountability is a must.

Darin: People want to collaborate but are suspicious. They are hesitant to become involved that much.

Francis: I believe it's important for people who work together to have regular times for prayer and Bible study. The style of such prayer and study should itself be collaborative. That joyful fatigue would strengthen them to be able to deal with conflict within and beyond the congregation.

Ray: I'm beginning to feel better about myself in being aware of the different ways I can deal with conflict. I no longer see conflict just as a personal attack but as a disconnection between two or more people. For example, last week I had to work with someone whom I do not enjoy working with, and, frankly, despise at times. I think these feelings are mutual. Throughout the afternoon we both let go of some control so the potential competition did not arise and we were able to collaborate. In the end, we both left feeling positive about the event and each other. We may never be friends but we now know that if need be, we are able to work together.

Bill: I believe I am changing, too. I believe conflict had some degree of control over me and thus limited my ability to reach out to others. Pastors and lay leaders often feel frozen into conflict avoidance or burned-out by allowing conflict to take its toll physically and emotionally. Viewing conflict through the cross provides a powerful, ironic, life-giving force for dealing with conflict.

Alan: Collaboration, it seems to me, has at least two crucial elements: mutual trust and open communication. Trust takes time *and* effort. In an effective collaborative relationship I was part of, we spoke openly until we understood each other. If we didn't agree, we at least were able to respect the other for his alternate point of view. The congregation noticed our relationship. I think this was a ministry in itself to a congregation that had been torn by conflict. We modeled for them a caring and trusting working relationship.

Marie: In a trusting relationship, I believe we start living more truly as who we were created to be: walking together, sharing ideas, discerning roles, honestly facing conflict, processing together, supporting, and validating one another even during times of disagreement.

Faith Reflections

Labor is part of life. Collaboration is essential for life together in Christian community. God created and it was good. God worked and then God rested (Gen. 1). We cannot create calm out of chaos, but as human stewards and as an anecdote to our intent to dominate and our proven record of dissension, our call to co-labor with God holds promise and calls for responsibility. We have been created for interdependence globally. In being reconciled with God in Jesus Christ, we have been reconciled with one another. We are called to collaborative ways of working through conflict and to work for restorative justice.[9] We will need to help create and sustain churchwide, ecumenical, interfaith, and international ways to co-labor, to resolve conflict in a world—in churches—crying out for peace.

Labor for New Life

A biblical word for strenuous labor is *travail*. A dictionary first meaning of the word is "physical or mental exertion," with the second meaning being "tribulation or distress," apt descriptions of what conflict and work together with it feels like. A third meaning of *travail* in *Webster's* is "the labor of childbirth."[10] Of the two dozen uses of *travail* in scripture, almost all of them are references to a woman in the anguish of giving birth (for example, John 16:21: "When a woman is in labor, she has pain, because her hour has come. But when her child is born, she no longer remembers the anguish because of the joy of having brought a human being into the world."), or comparing the anguish and the crying out of someone or some people *to* that of a woman in labor (for example, Isaiah 21:3; 42:14). God also *hears* the cry of God's people (for example, Jeremiah 4:31: "I heard a cry as of a woman in labor [travail], anguish as of one bringing forth her first child, the cry of daughter Zion gasping for breath, stretching our her hands").

The role of midwife was essential in standing by a woman in travail (for example, Genesis 35:16, 17: "Then they journeyed from Bethel; and when they were still some distance from Ephrath, Rachel was in childbirth, and she had hard labor. When she was in her hard labor [the phrase is repeated] the midwife said to her, 'Do not be afraid' "). The word *travail*, which means, "to labor," comes from the same root word as *travel*.[11] Travel is laborious, much more so in places without adequate transportation. That connection provides a helpful image of collaboration as the work of traveling together toward a destination. There is an end, perhaps in sight, perhaps not, to our laborious journey through conflict toward a place of new life together in Christ.

Likewise today, midwifery can be an appropriate image for the role of helping people through the painful work of conflict. We cannot give birth for another, but we can be there; we can struggle with them and guide them through the danger. We can help a whole people cry out to God in anguish and say, "Do not be afraid." There is no way back; there is no way except through the conflict, with the promise of birth and new life.

New Testament Hope

In Romans 8:22, we read that the whole creation has been groaning in labor pains. The entire text, Romans 8:18-39, is a powerful one for congregations working together through conflict, for it deals with suffering and hope, weakness and prayer. The Spirit intercedes. In the midst of stress, even persecution, nothing can separate us from God's love.

In the middle of this text is a verse too often quoted out of context, "All things work together for good for those who love God" (Romans 8:28*a*). Co-laboring in the midst of conflict cannot be so easily brushed off. Nor will it usually so quickly be resolved. The whole creation groans in labor pains. So often a whole church groans in labor pains. Only through Christ's death and resurrection (vv. 33-34) can we finally say, "For I am convinced that neither death, nor life, nor angels, nor rulers, nor things present, nor things to come, nor powers, nor height, nor depth, nor anything else in all creation, will be able to separate us from the love of God in Christ Jesus our Lord" (Romans 8:38-39).

The three Body of Christ passages in the New Testament—Romans 12, 1 Corinthians 12, and Ephesians 4—provide a living metaphor of collaborative ministry. We have different gifts and various functions, but we are members one of another (Romans 12:4, 5). Even when a community is split apart through dissension, members of Christ's Body are still joined together, and all needed. When we are tempted to say, "I'm out of here," 1 Corinthians 12:15 reminds us, "If the foot would say, 'Because I am not a hand, I do not belong to the body,' that would not make it any less a part of the body." In the midst of heated controversy we are tempted to dismiss others, and even try to get rid of them. First Corinthians 12:21 speaks loud and clear: "The eye cannot say to the hand, 'I have no need of you,' nor again the head to the feet, 'I have no need of you.'" And finally: "But speaking the truth in love, we must grow up in every way into him who is the head, into Christ, from whom the whole body, joined and knit together by every ligament with which it is equipped, as each part is working properly, promotes the body's growth in building itself up in love" (Ephesians 4:15, 16). Through all members of the Body working together, even, maybe particularly, through conflict, the Body is strengthened. [12]

Collaboration is essential for life together in communities of faith. We confess in the Apostles' Creed, "I believe in the Holy

Spirit, the holy catholic Church, the communion of saints, the forgiveness of sins." We do not work in vain when we choose collaboration as a response to conflict and when we help create sustainable collaborative ways of living as forgiven and forgiving people of God.

Personal Reflection

Take time to think back to the various responses to conflict about which you have read. (If you have read only the parts of the book that you thought related most directly to your situation, you might now wish to read the other chapters.) Are there some that were least favored that you now wish to try? Are there new possibilities that you would like to explore? How have you changed in reflecting on your own history with conflict? What new growth would you like to begin?

Collegial Conversation

Give thanks for one another. In the midst of conflict, we trouble one another. In the cross and resurrection of Christ we can now see one another not as burdens, but as gifts. Plan some ongoing regular time for conversation, for rituals of forgiving, and for collaboratively envisioning God's promised future.

Notes

1. There are many other collaborative relationships to which churches are called. See for example Elizabeth T. Boris and C. Eugene Steuerle, *Nonprofits and Government: Collaboration and Conflict* (Washington, D.C.: Urban Institute, 1999).

2. Teaching children methods of collaboration to respond to conflict is essential. See *Teaching Tolerance,* a magazine published by the Southern Poverty Law Center, 400 Washington Ave., Montgomery, AL 36104, and Carol Miller Lieber, *Partners in Learning: From Conflict to Collaboration in Secondary Classrooms* (Cambridge, Mass.: Educators for Social Responsibility, 2002).

3. Michael Koehler and Jeanne C. Baxter, *Leadership Through Collaboration* (Larchmont, N.Y.: Eye on Education, 1997). This book shares specific stories of school systems that have incorporated collaborative styles

of leadership. The authors note that "collaboration," "empowerment," "shared," and "participative" have been recurring buzzwords for decades, but that in order for them to replace oppressive and entrenched hierarchy, collaboration needs to be well integrated and internally consistent (p. 1).

4. Speed B. Leas, *Discover Your Conflict Management Style* (Washington, D.C.: Alban, 1997), pp. 20-23.

5. Joyce L. Hocker and William W. Wilmot, *Interpersonal Conflict,* 6th ed. (Boston: McGraw-Hill, 2001), p. 162.

6. See Stewart Levine, *Getting to Resolution: Turning Conflict into Collaboration* (San Francisco: Berrett Koehler, 1998). This book, written for the business and professional world, states simply that conflict, particularly the scars from the losing of a win-lose approach, is expensive. "Productivity and satisfaction, in business and personal relationships, comes from our ability to collaborate with others" (p. 5). Among Levine's ten principles for collaboration are: believing in abundance; being creative; fostering resolution; forming long-term collaborations; learning through the resolution process; and becoming responsible (pp. 43-94).

7. Process developed by Reverend Andrew Wendle, Trinity Lutheran Church, 2021 Northeast 19th Street, Gresham, OR 97030. Telephone: (503) 710-7409. Sources: www.spiritucc.org/governance/consesus.html; a resource of Spirit of the Lakes United Christian Church, Minneapolis, MN; www.decisionbridges.com/index.htm; www.users.vance.net/oumc/decision.htm; a resource by Alan Swartz for Oxford United Methodist Church, 1997.

8. Model of decision by consensus adopted by the Central Committee of Diakonia of the Americas and the Caribbean. This ecumenical group revised their constitution and bylaws to replace voting except where required for legal reasons or when consensus cannot be reached.

9. See John W. De Gruchy, *Reconciliation: Restoring Justice* (Minneapolis: Fortress Press, 2002). De Gruchy concludes his book with the chapter "Covananting Together to Restore Justice" (pp. 181-213).

10. *Webster's II New Riverside Desk Dictionary* (Boston: Houghton Mifflin, 1988), 439. Interestingly, by 1995 *Webster's Dictionary and Thesaurus,* a larger volume, no longer included the word *travail.*

11. Eric Partridge, *Origins* (New York: Macmillan, 1958), p. 735; Middle English, "travellen."

12. See George Cladis, *Leading the Team-based Church* (San Francisco: Jossey-Bass, 1999). Cladis uses the Body of Christ model of developing the varieties of gifts, services, and activities but the same Spirit, showing how to identify and learn from dysfunction in the body and to build team accountability (pp. 88-105).